NINE YEAR MIRACLE

THE CALEB LUCAS STORY

CATHYLEEN WILLIAMS

CONTENTS

Cover Design: Bridgette Gray

Editors: Kymberly Aviles, Jaenay McMillan, Cee McNeilus, Dwayne Rodgers, Cathyleen Williams

Printed in the United States of America

To my children:
Ashley and Caleb, you both are the two greatest gifts
God could have ever blessed me with.
I can't even put into words how thankful I am
That God allowed me to be your mother.
I know this life isn't easy, but I am so grateful
That I had the two of you and I would not
Change one moment for the world.
You both are such a blessing!

1

BEGINNING

I was 35 when I found out that I was pregnant, and John and I couldn't have been more thrilled! The very thought of bringing another life into the world was extremely exciting, considering the fact that we had just suffered a devastating miscarriage the previous year. We saw this as an opportunity to recover from our loss and I was determined to do everything I could to ensure that it resulted in a full-term pregnancy. I faithfully attended all of my appointments and strictly adhered to the doctor's instructions. It was during the 16th week ultrasound that we would be finding out if we were having a boy or a girl and the anticipation was absolutely overwhelming. We waited anxiously as the ultrasound tech checked all of the organs and measured the spine to ensure our baby was perfect. The moment came, and she finally revealed that we were having a baby boy! We couldn't believe what we were hearing, a baby boy! We became even more excited and all I could think was a son, we couldn't wait to get home and share the news with his big sister Ashley.

During the first three months of pregnancy, my body repeatedly attempted to push my son out which resulted in me being put on progesterone inserts that would stop my cervix from contracting. I was told by Dr. T to take it easy so that I wouldn't lose the baby. Earlier that year my husband's grandfather had passed away and we were by no means mentally or physically prepared to suffer any additional loss. She also informed me that although I was in good health, due to my age coupled with a history of miscarriages, my pregnancy was considered high risk and she wanted me to see a Chromosomal Specialist.

After receiving the referral from Dr. T, I reluctantly scheduled a consultation with Dr. S. My husband and I were both dreading the appointment because of the potential bad news we could receive. After all, with everything else that had recently gone wrong in our lives, the only thing we wanted to hear at this point was good news. When we arrived at our appointment we were extremely anxious. We prayed for the best and prepared mentally for the worst.

Waiting for the doctor seemed like an eternity and when he finally entered, it felt as if every ounce of oxygen left the room. He performed an ultrasound and stated that the purpose was to reveal any abnormalities. As the word abnormalities left his lips we noticed a change in his facial expression. To my astonishment, John blurted out the very questions that I was pondering in my mind. What's the matter? What do you see? Dr. S said that my son's kidneys were slightly full and that they weren't draining properly. Thankfully, he followed up with it and it wasn't uncommon in boy's and sometimes their ureters are stiff and once they're born the issue normally resolves itself. To further ease our minds, he also stated that if it didn't there was a minor surgery that would correct it. We were a little concerned with the thought of our newborn baby going into surgery even if it was considered just a minor procedure. Needless to say, the ride home was a quiet one as our fears presented the ultimate challenge to our faith. As I looked out of my window I silently prayed and asked the Lord to please heal my little man and fix the issue with his kidneys. Amen.

The 28 weeks were unremarkable, and we were keeping in step with all of our appointments and monitoring his kidneys very closely. During that time, we were trying to pick a name but were unable to decide on one. While pondering on all of the adversity that we were facing the thought came to me that we must name him Caleb! It means faithful one and the bible story of Caleb and Joshua is an amazing adventure about two young men who lead the Israelites into the Promised Land. It also speaks of how although there were giants in the land they were to occupy, they remained fearless and said with great confidence, let's go and possess the land God has promised us. The name Caleb was the perfect selection. I could see him becoming the new beginning that our family needed and was absolutely certain that he would bring joy and happiness to us all.

My next appointment with Dr. S was on August 3, 2006, I was approximately 31 weeks (I will never forget because it was my grandfather's birthday) and the doctor scanned everything as usual. To our surprise Caleb's kidney issue had resolved itself. We were so relieved with such great news that John felt empowered to ask if all of his other organs and spine were alright. The doctor said you have a healthy little boy who is progressing very nicely. With hearts filled with joy, the car ride home was nothing short of a party overflowing with happiness and thanks to God for healing Caleb.

As the delivery date drew closer, because of my age and surrounding circumstances my OB doctor wanted to begin conducting stress tests. I willingly agreed and attended weekly testing of which everything was going just fine. That was until a hysterical pregnant woman came rolling through giving birth in a wheelchair. My stress levels went through the roof when I noticed that the baby was already halfway out, so much to the point that I started having contractions. I called John and told him I had started early labor and he came there immediately. My OB doctor rushed in and said you are a little too early to go into labor and I want you to get an ultrasound to see if there is adequate fluid and how the baby is doing. As the tech was scanning Caleb we got a full view of his face. That was the first time we had ever seen Caleb because he would always hide. We were in such amazement that we finally got to see our baby boy's face. Afterwards I was wheeled back to my room where the nurse asked me when I was scheduled to see the specialist again. We thought it was rather odd because we had just seen him, and he told us that our son was fine. The nurse said we were free to leave but that Dr. T would be calling us shortly to go over the results with us. This left us both feeling uncertain and afraid of what Dr. T could possibly have to tell us now?

At home the time seemed to stand still. We continued staring at the phone waiting for it to ring, but not really wanting it to ring. We wanted answers, yet we were afraid of what the answers might be. The phone finally rang, and it was Dr. T. She told us that after carefully reviewing the ultrasound that Caleb's kidneys were fine but that unfortunately there was something wrong with his heart, and that we needed a return visit to Dr. S. We were in shock, Dr. S had just told us in August that our baby boy was fine. He was healthy then, and now, according to the information we were still trying to process, there was something wrong with his heart. How could this be? In between being in disbelief and sobbing uncontrollably I scheduled an appointment with Dr. S. I was lucky enough to get the appointment for the very next day. I was so scared and couldn't stop crying because of all the different scenarios racing through my mind of what could possibly be wrong with my baby.

The next day we drove to the chromosomal doctor's office for another scan. The doctor confirmed that there indeed were some abnormalities in Caleb's heart. He suggested we see a pediatric cardiologist for a fetal echocardiogram. He also suggested a colleague that would be able to get us in the next day but that his office was three hours away from our home. At that point we didn't care about distance we needed answers, so we told the doctor we would take that appointment. Our whole word felt like it was crumbling around us. It was just confirmed that Caleb had something wrong with his heart. That night was extremely difficult. We were having such a hard time wrapping our minds around exactly what was taking place. Like so many others I made the mistake of Googling a few things which only complicated matters and made the situation worse. I just could not stop crying.

The next morning, we made our way to the pediatric cardiologist to get a fetal echocardiogram. John and I were so scared, and we didn't talk much because we were in disbelief that all of this was even happening. The tech did the echo which seemed to be moving in slow motion. I didn't even look at the screen, I just kept praying and pleading the blood of Jesus over Caleb. She told me she was done and that she had all the pictures she needed and that the doctor would be in shortly to go over the echo. I was so nervous, all I could keep saying was God hath not given me the spirit of fear but of power, love and a sound mind. Finally, after what seemed like forever the doctor came in and went over the results. He said that Caleb had a heart defect called Hypoplastic Left Heart Syndrome and that in layman's terms our son only had half of a heart. The whole left side of his heart had not developed. He then went on to explain what that meant for Caleb as well as for us. We were devastated, and all we could do was cry. Our hearts were broken at the realization that our sweet, little, baby boy would literally be in a fight for his life. The cardiologist went over our options with us. He said we had three to choose from. Option one would be a heart transplant and unfortunately most babies die waiting for the heart because infant hearts don't become available often. Option two was a three-stage surgery called the Norwood procedure. He went into great detail of what the surgeries consisted of. If we choose this option Caleb's first open heart surgery would be in the first few days after birth and he noted that although most babies have a difficult time with the changes, some however do really well and adapt. The last option which was actually no option for us at all was simply to allow Caleb to die. The doctor explained he would only live a few days because his body wouldn't be able to sustain his life. Those were our options and John and I were both now left with the unavoidable task of deciding the fate of our child.

My prenatal care was instantly changed to Loma Linda Children's hospital. I was transferred to a new OBGYN and had to have several new tests ran. They performed another fetal echocardiogram and suggested we go see the NICU and the CVICU so that we could see what Caleb would look like when he was born. I felt so nervous walking in and seeing all those little babies hooked up to various apparatuses. I couldn't fathom how this could possibly be good for us. We both tried so hard to be brave but deep down inside it was the hardest thing we'd ever done. They were so little and fragile with tiny frames that were attached to what appeared to be a sea of wires leading to machines with alarms that repeatedly sounded. It was at that very moment that it really hit us that the life we had once known would become non-existent and forever changed. Once again, the silence of the long ride home was deafening at the rationalization that our skin to skin moments with our soon to be newborn Caleb would be replaced with machines, constant monitoring and a series of surgeries.

I continued to keep my appointments as Caleb's birth approached. John and I made the only sensible decision and chose option two which was the three-stage surgery. The other two options weren't even something we would consider. At least this way Caleb would have a fighting chance at life. Upon completion of all of the newly requested tests, the doctor briefed us on the results. He stated that Caleb had moderate Hypoplastic

Left Heart Syndrome which made the diagnosis sound as not as severe as it actually was. We were encouraged when he explained that once the surgery was performed the left side of his heart would help with the overall functionality.

The next few weeks were so hard. We tried to get back to some sense of normalcy, but it was practically impossible. It got so bad that I prayed to God, literally begged Him to take my son so he wouldn't have to come into this world. I cried out in tears, "Lord please have mercy on my baby Caleb." I didn't want him to experience the struggles that awaited him if he were to enter this world. As horrible as that may have seemed my heart just wanted Caleb to go back to Heaven where he'd be safe in my Father's arms. It was at that moment that I came to the conclusion that with all that was going on there was absolutely no way that I could give adequate attention to the issues of everyday life as well as take care of Caleb. I had no other choice but to stop working and drop out of school.

In spite of me pleading with God from a deep place of sincerity to not allow Caleb to come forth, He didn't grant my petition and on October 19th, 2006 I began having contractions. Although they were happening every fifteen minutes I tried my best to remain calm. I knew that once Caleb came out he'd need to be at the hospital so that he could get the intensive care he needed. Barstow was quite far from Loma Linda, CA so I had John drive me there just to be safe. We went to the ER and they sent me straight to the OB unit. Once there the doctor's checked me and said I was only dilated two centimeters. They monitored me for a little while and said I wasn't in active labor and that they were going to send me home. We were so upset and explained to them what was going on with Caleb and that he had a terminal heart defect. Can you believe it? They still sent me home. Needless to say, John and I were extremely upset. By that time, I was having contractions every 5 minutes and was stressed like never before. When we arrived home we both were exhausted and decided that the best option was to get some rest.

John slept like a baby as I labored all night. The next day we went for walks repeatedly, but nothing seemed to help. John went to work that night but around 3 am I couldn't take it anymore I told him he had to get me back to the hospital. Once we were there my OB doctor checked me and I had only progressed to a three. I couldn't believe it, after all the laboring I thought I had done. I asked him if I could have an epidural because I was hurting and so tired. He explained all the anesthesiologists were busy and that they would get to me as soon as they could. I was so tired, so he gave me a little something to take the edge off. Unfortunately, that didn't last very long, and I was back to experiencing contractions every 5 minutes. I wasn't progressing, so the OB doctor said he would need to start me on some medication that would help me to dilate. Of course, once it was hooked up, my contractions started coming stronger and more frequently. Finally, at 11 am the anesthesiologist came and was ready to give me an epidural. Believe me, after three days of labor I couldn't thank him enough. I wasn't even afraid of the needle entering into my spine. I was so exhausted from the contractions I couldn't wait to be out of pain and hopefully get a little rest before Caleb decided to make his appearance. By the time I was done receiving the epidural, family and friends had started showing up to the hospital. The news of Caleb coming was exciting and terrifying all at the same time as we had no idea what to expect once Caleb was born.

I must say that the doctors were very vigilant with monitoring everything. They had all of their equipment set and ready for any situation that might present itself once Caleb was out of my womb. There were countless people coming in and out of my room. There was even a group of students that stopped by to observe. The head doctors were explaining what was going on and what Caleb's heart defect was. They also discussed different scenarios that could come into play once he was delivered. I remember a few student's asking if they could examine me as they had never felt a dilated cervix before. I was so tired I really didn't care what they did as long as I could go back to sleep. When one of the students checked me, my water broke, and I felt so bad. If you could have seen the look on his face it was priceless. Once my water broke the contractions were stronger than ever with some hitting so hard they made Caleb's heart rate drop. The room got frantic, the doctor's thought they were going to have to do an emergency C-section, but because of my fast-acting nurse I didn't have to have one. She reduced the medication dosage and the intensity of the contractions subsided which in return normalized Caleb's heart rate. As the feeling started to return to my mid-section I felt Caleb's head drop into the birth canal. It was time to push and bring him into this world. The room was filled with rampant, running emotions due to us all being scared and excited at the same time. The doctors were geared up and ready for Caleb to make his appearance. It was time to push and with the next contraction Caleb's head came out. I was so on edge and praying that Caleb would be ok. The second contraction came, and I tried to push his shoulders out, but I was unsuccessful. As I felt a third one coming on

I began to bare down and push again. I did it, I got his shoulders out! There was our little Caleb out and into the doctor's hands.

Before Caleb was born the doctors had warned us that Caleb probably wouldn't be crying or even able to breath on his own depending on how his heart function was. Praise God, Caleb came out screaming at the top of his little lungs. Once John cut the umbilical cord the doctor's whisked him right away. They needed to check Caleb out to make sure he was breathing properly and how his heart was performing. Everyone diverted their attention from me and went directly over to Caleb. I repeatedly asked, "Is he ok, is he ok?" but I received no answer. The room was full of hospital personnel performing various tasks. Once the doctors finished checking Caleb out they got him cleaned up and let John hold him first. There were tears of joy and fear as we had no idea what was in store. The moment came when I was able to finally hold Caleb. I can remember being in awe of my son. He looked so perfect! Like any other baby but the reality was he wasn't. He was so little but so handsome, 6 pounds and 19 ½ inches long.

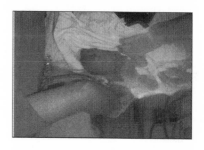

I wanted to fall in love with him, but I was so afraid to allow my heart to be vulnerable. I kissed him and cried thinking how bitter and sweet this moment was. They took Caleb away from me, put him in the islet, and rushed him to the NICU. All I could do was cry, I was trying to wrap my mind around all that had just happened. I prayed that the Lord would be with my precious little boy and that God would give wisdom to the doctor's on exactly what to do to give him the life he deserved to have. Once he was taken to the NICU the doctors came back and told us it would be a while before we could see him. They explained how the next time we saw Caleb he would be hooked up to all those wires just like the babies we had saw before when we visited the NICU.

At last I was able to get something to eat! I was so hungry I hadn't eaten in days! As I was finishing up eating, the doctors said Caleb was ready and we could go see him. They escorted us to where Caleb was, and my heart sank when I saw him connected to all those machines. The nurses immediately asked me if I wanted to hold him and I reluctantly declined. I was so afraid I was going to hurt him. The nurses were great at explaining what all the wires were as well as going over the different medications Caleb was receiving. It was so much to take in and I became overwhelmed and began to cry uncontrollably. The nurse gently explained that babies feed off of their parent's energy and that it was best for me to step away and cry. After regaining my composure, I returned back to his bedside.

During our visit at the NICU the nurses asked me if I was going to breastfeed Caleb. I had already determined that I would do so because I knew that it was best for him especially under the circumstances. To my surprise I found out I would be pumping instead of feeding naturally because Caleb wasn't allowed to eat yet because they needed to monitor him for a bit. That's when we learned we would have to keep track of everything going in and coming out of Caleb. The nurse brought me a feeding kit and I pumped every 3 hours to ensure that Caleb would have plenty of breast milk fortified with all the antibodies he needed to survive. I knew how important it was for babies to receive their mother's milk, but for Caleb it was even more so because within the next few days he would be going in for his first open heart surgery.

The next few days were like a roller coaster filled with many ups and downs. Caleb had been doing well until the medications simply became too much for him and caused difficulty with his breathing. This required him to be put on CPAP (Continuous Positive Airway Pressure), which helped keep positive pressure in his airways to assist with breathing. Unfortunately, the insurance policy only covered the hospital stay for two days and I would be required to leave. I was devastated when I found out that the Ronald McDonald house was full and therefore I had no choice but to return home and leave my baby boy. That was so difficult, I felt like I was abandoning him. John and I wrestled with this decision but due to the strain that my body had already endured from having Caleb we both decided it be best for me to go home. We prayed over Caleb and headed out. I was saddened but I was also aware that I had to get myself together because in the next few days Caleb would be having surgery and fighting for his life.

John went to work that night and I tried to rest. I called the hospital several times throughout the night checking on Caleb. I kept apologizing to the nurse and I explained I was scared and just needed to know he was ok. My mind and body were exhausted from everything that I had been through both physically and emotionally. My daughter Ashley was also having a hard time taking in everything that was going on. I tried to comfort her but who was I kidding, I was in desperate need of comforting myself. We were all frightened that Caleb would never come home and that we'd be robbed of the chance to love him. It was very hard on me to be at home when everything in me wanted to be at the hospital with Caleb. Although I was torn with conflict within I know that my body needed to rest and recover.

I received a call from a 909 number and my heart dropped. Immediately I thought it was the hospital calling me to tell me that something was wrong with Caleb. But to my surprise it was the Ronald McDonald house. They called to tell me that there was a room for us. It couldn't have come at a better time because Caleb's surgery was just two days away. I hung up the phone praising God for blessing us with a room at just the right time. I was so happy that I would be closer and able to spend more time with Caleb. I got my bags ready and once John woke up we headed there to check in.

Once we arrived at the Ronald McDonald house we were buzzed in and greeted by a guide. The facility was absolutely gorgeous as well as thoughtfully designed to accommodate every need that a family could possibly have. It had a community kitchen and also washers and dryers for residents to utilize. There was even a cupboard of our very own where we could store food. The guide also informed us that occasionally local restaurants and organizations come in and prepare dinner for the families. She then directed our attention to a chalkboard in the dinner area that indicated when they were scheduled to come. We continued our tour and the first stop was the backyard which was covered with toys and lots of interesting things for the children to do. The next stop was the library and then on to a playroom that included the latest video games. It was so amazing to know that something like that was set up for the sole purpose of helping families in a time of their greatest need. The finale was us being escorted to our room and given the keys to our new temporary residence. We were humbled by the entire experience and reflected on how we were blessed to have the privilege of lodging in such a nice facility. Now that the lodging situation was no longer an issue, it was off to the hospital to see Caleb.

Once there, John and I were both doing our best to be supportive while attempting to simultaneously learn all of the different processes required to care for Caleb. At the time it seemed like an informational overload and I felt that my brain was going to literally shut down at any moment. I must admit that deep within I was extremely afraid and wrestled with holding Caleb due to the fear that I would somehow hurt him. There were so many wires and machines attached to my precious baby boy that just the sight of it caused a constant stream of tears to flow down my face. Caleb was unable to feed for the first two days, so it was a relief when the doctor's decided to allow him, due to him becoming stable and now weaned from the CPAP. He was doing absolutely amazing so the doctor's set a goal to get him feeding from a bottle. This was very exciting news! Caleb did very well with his feedings and therefore it allowed his intake amounts to be increased. Before we knew it, he was feeding from a bottle. The nurse warned us that sometimes after an open-heart surgery which requires the heart and lung bypass machine, babies oftentimes forget how to suckle. We found that to be discouraging but looked on the brighter side of at least he was doing it for now and making great progress. Caleb was doing so well and seemed to be getting stronger day by day. I began feeling more comfortable and hope began to arise that we would make it through this and be okay. I finally got the nerve up and decided to hold Caleb.

Surprisingly, I wasn't even afraid of the wires or the machines any longer. I had fallen completely in love with him and wanted to shower him with every bit of affection that I could. It was at that moment that the love in my heart for my baby overcame the fear of everything that I was seeing with my eyes.

During the days leading up to the surgery we had many talks with doctor's as they tried to prepare us for what was coming and what we were to expect if indeed Caleb survived the surgery. They painted two very real pictures. One was that of what things would be like if everything turned out perfect. The other picture was of the disappointment we may encounter and possibly even the harsh reality that Caleb may not recover from or even survive shortly after surgery. It was hard for us both to accept that in just a few days our son would have his first open heart surgery. The doctor's advised us to get plenty of rest because we needed to be ready for the things we would encounter. We would be facing long days, filled with various events as well as unpredictable emotions. It was the night before Caleb's first open heart surgery and he had come so far and was doing so well. I was in awe of the Lord and how he had already performed so many miracles in Caleb's little five days of being in existence. As I sat there holding him tightly I began to sing to him Jesus loves the little children. I didn't want to let him go, let alone leave him as I was so uncertain of what the next day would bring. The sobering reality set in that it might be my last day I'd ever be able to hold my son. I had let my guard down and fallen head over heels in love with this little boy who only had half a heart, the reality was that Caleb had actually stolen my whole heart. How was I going to put him down when I knew that it could possibly be the last moment I'd spend with him. John and I were both torn and trying so hard to hold back our tears. We then whispered a prayer and reluctantly put him back in his islet. We knew we needed to try and get some rest because we had a big day if front of us.

On October 27, 2006 Caleb went in for his first open heart

surgery. He was the first case, so we were up and at the hospital bright and early. The team of doctors came in and had us sign release forms and once again discussed what Caleb's surgery entailed. Signing the papers was one of the hardest things I'd ever had to do in my life. I knew once they were signed I'd have to release him. Release him to a surgery where there was absolutely no guarantee that he would ever return. Just the thought of them cutting his chest wide open made me want to just take my baby and run away. I wanted to run as far away as possible from that place to where no one could hurt him, and he would be safe, but the reality was there was no where I could go to make that happen. The truth was if I didn't allow them to take him and perform the surgery then Caleb would have indeed died. There were no other options at that point, there was no turning back. Caleb had to go if I ever wanted to have some kind of future, some kind of life with my son. The uncertainty weighed so heavily. How? How did we get here and how were we ever going to be able to make it through this?

Now it was time! The doctors were ready to take Caleb in for his first open-heart surgery called the Norwood Procedure. The medical team began to surround Caleb's bed. They unlocked the wheels and prepared him for transport to the surgery area. We were told that we could come with them to the surgery ward but there would be a door we would have to stop at and that's where we wouldn't be permitted to go any further. His surgeon came to the room preparing to take Caleb for surgery. He asked if he could whisper a word of prayer so that God would guide his hands and mind exactly for what was needed to be done so that Caleb could live. How awesome was that! Dr. R wanted to pray God's will over Caleb and that God would lead him. At that moment I loved Dr. R so much and gave him a big hug. He began to pray, and I must admit that the prayer was both empowering and frightening all at the same time. It also reminded me that God was in control of everything and that His will would be done in Caleb's life. As the prayer concluded, we proceeded towards where the surgery would be performed. The medical team kept hugging me and reassuring us that they would do everything in their power to ensure Caleb's safety. We arrived at the elevators and just waited. My heart was racing, and I felt like I was going to throw up. We entered the brightly lit space, and someone hit the button and we descended down to the surgery ward. We were only on the elevator for a few short moments, but it was as if time had stood still. We were all looking at Caleb. I was trying to be strong for my baby, but the truth is I was a nervous wreck. I kept telling myself that I could do it but internally my heart was shattering into a thousand pieces. I stiffened my lips to appear to be unmoved, but silently I screamed in desperation to awaken from this nightmare. The elevator came to a halt, and the doors slowly opened. As we exited I got the chills because it was so cold. We proceeded down the hall and eventually arrived at an area that reeked of bleach. As we came to a halt our eyes transitioned from Caleb to the closed doors that stood before us. The moment of truth had arrived, and reality came crashing down like a ton of bricks. My precious little boy was going in to his first open heart surgery. Everything went numb and it felt like my legs were going to give out. I stood paralyzed with fear as I gave a last-ditch effort to hold back the tears. I couldn't allow my emotions to get the best of me, I knew Caleb would be able to sense it. As they departed, John and I whispered another word of prayer over Caleb as we showered him with kisses and told him how much we loved him. We stood there alone as we watched the doors slowly close behind them, not knowing if we would ever make eye contact with our precious baby boy again.

I was consumed with guilt and couldn't help but feel that I had just sent my son off to the wolves. At that moment the realization sunk in that I had absolutely no control over what the outcome would be. I attempted to put all of my faith and trust in God, but in all honesty, I wasn't even sure if I possibly could under the circumstances. I was terrified that I wouldn't see Caleb again. As John and I headed back up the elevator we cried and held each other tightly, we both so desperately needed to be consoled. Upon exiting the elevator into the waiting room, I collapsed into John's arms and began wailing so loudly that one of the nurses walking by heard me. She rushed and wrapped her arms around me and immediately started praying for the Lord to comfort me. She asked the Lord to grant me the peace He referred to in the Bible that only He can give. She continued praying asking Him to surround me with His angels and for Caleb's strength to withstand the storm of the surgery. She also prayed for the doctor's that He would guide their hands for whatever His will was for Caleb's life. In closing she prayed for John that he would have the wisdom and strength to lead our family. She then asked me if I trusted God. I replied yes, of course I do! She replied good because you must trust Him with all your heart and soul right now and know that He has Caleb's best interest at hand whatever the outcome may be. I gave her a heartfelt hug and thanked her so much for praying with us.

We made our way to the waiting room where we literally sat for hours. We finally got an update from one of the nurses but since she spoke using medical terminology we were oblivious to exactly what was being conveyed. The only portion we really understood was that Caleb was stable and doing well and that was all we needed to hear. The time seemed to go by so slow, every time I looked at the clock hoping Caleb would be done, only a few minutes had passed. We were told by the doctors that the surgery would take anywhere from 6 to 12 hours depending on how Caleb's body responded, but I don't think it resonated until now. Finally, we got the call we had been waiting for, Caleb was done and would be back in his room in 45 minutes. John and I started crying uncontrollably and hugging each other. We were overjoyed that Caleb had made it through the surgery. Praise God He had answered our prayers.

We were directed to a room where the doctor would brief us on Caleb's surgery. John and I went in and waited for him. We held each other's hand tightly as we readied ourselves for what he would have to say. We wanted to be optimistic about everything, but at the same time we didn't want to fool ourselves. We knew that Caleb had been through a lot given the fact that he only had half of a heart. We sat there waiting to the point that the anticipation became unbearable. That 45 minutes seemed like forever when finally, Dr. R came into the room. He looked exhausted and proceeded to explain that Caleb's surgery was very successful and that everything went well. He said that Caleb seemed to be handling all of the changes well, and his heart was doing great. John and I started to cry, we couldn't believe it. That was the best news ever! Dr. R told us that the nurses were recovering Caleb and that we would be able to see our son very soon. He also said due to the severity of the type of surgery, although Caleb had done well the next 48 hours were crucial and that a lot could change for the better but also for the worse. John and I were relieved to hear that news, but at the same time apprehensive as we knew Caleb had a long road to recovery. Caleb was only six days old, only six pounds, and had just went through something most people in life never go through.

Dr. R exited, and we sat there trying to take everything in. The nurse entered the room and told us we could go in and see Caleb. I was scared and didn't want to go. I asked John if he would please go first and that way he could prepare me for what I'd be seeing. I was a coward, but my emotions were all over the place. I had just had Caleb six days before all of this. The conversation we had with the doctors before surgery about how Caleb could look very different after surgery came to mind. They'd explained that Caleb could be swollen to the point of being unrecognizable. Thankfully, John agreed and went first. I waited in the waiting room for him to return. While I sat there so many different thoughts raced through my mind. What did Caleb look like? What would life be like for him? What would life be like for the rest of us? Could we do this? Could we care for a very sick little boy?

John came out of the elevator after visiting with Caleb. As we locked eyes I attempted to read how he was genuinely feeling, not the edited version to make me feel better because he knew how torn up I was dealing with all of this. John's spirit was very light as he described how Caleb looked. He explained that Caleb looked exactly the same, but that there were more tubes hooked up to him than before in the NICU. The nurse had told him that Caleb had staples in his chest where the incision was made for his open-heart surgery, but John explained it wasn't that bad and that there was a bandage covering it. I was tearing up, so John wrapped his arms around me and said he knew I was scared but everything is going to be ok, together we would get through this. He encouraged me to go up and see Caleb and I agreed to go in with him the next time. The only stipulation would be that Caleb's chest be covered before me entering. I knew that might prove to be overwhelming for me.

The hour had passed, and it was time to go up and see Caleb again. As I stood silently on the elevator, the same emotions overcame me again. My heart was racing, and I trembled with fear. John hugged me and said don't worry babe everything is going to be alright, Caleb needed us to be strong. We exited the elevator and went up to the receptionist for the CVICU (Cardiovascular Intensive Care Unit). She called back and got the ok from the nurse and buzzed us in. Fear grasped my body again and John said wait right here and let me make sure they cover up Caleb's chest. I stood there so afraid and unable to even walk into the room. He came back out and reassured me that everything was ok. He took me by the hand and slowly led me into Caleb's room. The room was brightly lit with machines beeping everywhere. The nurse caring for Caleb kindly welcomed me in. She said please wash your hands before coming over to see Lucas to prevent passing any germs to him. We were used to that because down in the NICU we had to do the same thing. As I turned the water on at the sink, there was the smell of that soap again. I can't put into words what it smelled like, but I knew I didn't like it. I knew that germs were a big deal, but I had no idea how much of a threat they would be from here on out.

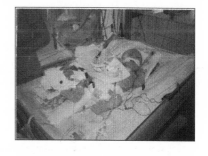

The nurse then formally introduced herself. She said in a very cheerful voice my name is Jennifer and immediately went over what all new lines were and what medication they had running in them. She also explained what each medication was for. She then told me that I could touch Caleb and not to be afraid. I conveyed to her I was scared and that if I did would I hurt him? She smiled and said no! I slowly went over to the islet where Caleb was laying and looked at him. I was trying so hard to get the courage up to touch my baby. I was over- whelmed with all that I was seeing and hearing and felt like I was going to pass out right there. I was trying to be brave, but I could feel the tears streaming down my face. Jennifer kindly reminded me that babies feed off of our energy and that although it may be difficult, I must remain strong especially when in Caleb's presence. In my mind I was thinking how on God's green earth could I do that. Did she not see what I was seeing? For the sake of Caleb and with a little self-pep talk I began to pull myself together. Our energy would be the thing that would help Caleb heal and expedite the recovery process. Jennifer explained Caleb also needed us to touch him and that babies thrive off interaction. Before we knew it, our fifteen minutes were up, and it was time for us to leave. John and I asked if we could say a prayer over Caleb and Jennifer replied of course. We asked her if there was anything specific we should pray for and she explained that his heart rate was a little high and she would like to see his numbers drop some. I know my face must have changed because she then immediately began to console me. She said it was not unusual after a surgery because they are trying to adjust to the changes and he may still be in some pain. The medications would also be adjusted to make sure things remained under control. That definitely was a relief and made so much sense. We invited her to pray with us and she said she would be delighted. We prayed specifically for his heart rate and then kissed him, told him how much we loved him and left his room.

As we left I thanked John for supporting me through the whole ordeal and told him that it wasn't that bad after all. Seeing Caleb like that wasn't easy, but for the moment I was thankful he was still here and that he made it through the surgery. Caleb was so strong, but I knew from here on out that he would have a serious fight on his hands. I genuinely dreaded that for him, so I cried out to the Lord as I had done so many times before asking God to have mercy on my little boy. This time the prayer was so different because I had fallen head over heels in love with Caleb. I prayed so hard asking God to heal him because I couldn't imagine life without him now. I prayed for the nurses and the staff that God would guide them in exactly what it would take to keep my son here on this earth because I couldn't bear to lose him.

John and I went back a few more times that evening. Each time before we would leave we would ask the nurse the things that she was most concerned with and that would be what we would pray for. The results from the prayers were amazing and probably a little unbelievable. Each time we returned for a follow up, God had answered our prayers and that very thing the nurse was concerned with had been resolved. We were experiencing the love of GOD first hand by Him hearing our prayers and answering them.

As the days went on we were learning more and more about the medications and how to take care of Caleb once we were home. When the time came to remove the bandage from Caleb's incision, I counted the staples and there was a total of thirteen embedded in his little chest. It was the craziest thing I had ever seen. He was just a new born baby and yet he had thirteen staples in his chest. Caleb was getting better, so they decided to attempt to remove the breathing tube to see if he could breathe on his own. Once again fear overtook me, but I knew it was time for me to be strong, so I could support Caleb in whatever was needed to get him well and home.

The nurse told us that the doctors would be in soon to remove the tube, so John and I prayed over Caleb asking the Lord to give him strength to be able to handle having the tube out. We prayed his lungs would be ready. The doctors came into the room and made preparations for the removal. They went over the details and what the best possible outcome could be, which was Caleb would be able to breath on his own. Then the worst-case scenario would be that his lungs weren't quite ready and that the tube would have to be reinserted. We left the room while they removed the tube and waited patiently in the lobby for about thirty minutes. I prayed for the doctors and especially for Caleb that he would be able to endure it.

The nurse came and got us, and we were able to return back to the room. Although Caleb was off of the breathing tube, he didn't look so well. As we moved closer to the islet I could see him struggling with every breath that he took. Caleb looked so uncomfortable. The nurse asked me if I wanted to hold him but because of the way he was breathing I declined the offer. Now that Caleb had the breathing tube out we no longer had to leave but with the turn of events that would occur shortly afterwards, I wish that we would have. Caleb's oxygen levels were dropping slowly, and he was turning a weird purple, grayish color. I began to panic as it unfolded right before my very eyes. The nurse ran a blood gas test and attempted to correct the imbalances but was unsuccessful, so the doctor decided to reinsert the breathing tube. It placed a major dampener on our high hopes for Caleb, but he simply just wasn't strong enough yet and the tube had to go back in.

Due to the stress on Caleb's body from the removal of the tube he became extremely weak. At that moment I was unsure if Caleb was going to make it. I must have asked the doctor's a million questions hoping they could help me really understand what was going on with my baby. I expressed all of my concerns but all of the doctor's reassured us that Caleb's body just wasn't quite ready yet. They decided to let his body rest and would try again in a few days. This unfortunately caused us to have to return to visiting only fifteen minutes each hour. We went every hour and I was so paranoid, I just wanted to be sure Caleb was ok. I began to feel fatigued as well as physically and mentally exhausted, but I couldn't bring myself to leave for fear that it would be the last time I saw Caleb. John finally put his foot down and said we were going back to the room to get some rest. He told the nurse that if anything changed to call us because we were just across the street at the Ronald McDonald house.

Two days later the doctor's decided that Caleb was ready for another attempt at taking the tube out. Here we go again. Questions jumbled around in my head such as would this go round be successful, or would it be like the last time. Once again, we prayed over Caleb and went out to the waiting area while they removed the tube. The nurse came out once they were done and told us we could see him. As we entered the room we weren't sure what to expect. We approached Caleb's islet and to our surprise Caleb was doing well. His O2 levels were exactly where they were supposed to be, and he was doing great thank God! He had made it through one more obstacle and God had sustained him.

Now we would be able to stay in the room for as long as we wanted. We no longer would have to leave. The nurse asked me once again if I wanted to hold Caleb and I immediately said yes. I couldn't wait to snuggle with my little angel. I sat anxiously in the rocking chair as the nurse got Caleb out of his bed and handed him to me. I could feel the tears rolling down my cheeks, not because I was scared but because I was so thankful I could finally hold my little Caleb. What a blessing to be able to embrace him once again. I was overjoyed and couldn't stop praising God for all that He had done for Caleb. As I rocked him I softly sang to him Jesus loves the little children. John was ready to hold him as well, but I must admit that I was being selfish and didn't want to let him go. We both enjoyed him being in the safety of his mommy's arms, but I needed to pump milk for Caleb, so it gave me an excuse to give John a turn.

As Caleb grew stronger and stronger we found out that the better you are the further back in the CVICU you are moved. The sicker babies needed to be up front. That was so encouraging, it meant Caleb was improving and that we were possibly on our way home. We were moved to a room that already had a baby in it and we had pleasure of meeting the parents. We introduced ourselves and the parent's told us that their baby's name was Lauren and that she and Caleb had similar heart defects. They had both underwent the same surgery as well. It was a pleasure meeting Lauren's parents, Camille and Race and I found it comforting conversing with others who could truly relate to what we were going through. Camille and I talked as if we had known each other for years. We went on and on about our precious babies and how they were only a few days apart and had already been through so much. We became pretty good friends and exchanged numbers to stay in contact.

As the days progressed Caleb's number of tubes became less and less. His medications were all transitioned from IV to oral administration. The nurses were teaching us the steps and precautions we would have to do once we got Caleb home and it was a bit overwhelming. In spite of it being so much information to process we were well aware that if we wanted Caleb to come home we had to learn it all. We had to precisely measure all of his intake as well as everything leaving his body because he had a shunt placed during surgery. Proper care would be critical because if Caleb were to become dehydrated the shunt could close and there would be a possibility of him dying.

The head nurse Irene was very thorough with our training. She gave us a folder of charts that would help us stay on course with managing his records. One would be utilized to keep track of medications and what time they were to be administered. Another to record his daily milk intake and yet another to track diaper usage. We were required to watch videos and learn to use a pulse-ox so that we could monitor his oxygen saturation and heart rate. We had to bring our CPR cards because if we weren't certified we would have to be before Caleb would be allowed to come home. Because he was still having a hard time sucking from the bottle and had a feeding tube in his nose, it was mandatory that we learn how to insert the tube in through his nose and down into his belly. On top of that it was essential that we be knowledgeable on how to check for placement to ensure that the tube was inserted correctly in his stomach. We were learning so much in such a short period of time. As if this weren't already enough going on I was still pumping every 3 hours. It was insane to think once we got home the medical staff wasn't going to be there and we would be on our own.

Although my body was still healing physically, emotionally I wasn't doing so well. I was literally exhausted from worrying about Caleb and him still having trouble with his feeds. We were trying to get him to eat like he did before surgery but because he was put on the Heart and lung bypass machine he was unable to. Each time Caleb would eat we would let him try the bottle for five to ten minutes and if he was unsuccessful we would gravity gavage the rest of the milk into stomach. Throughout this process John and I became proficient in feeding him through the tube. We would first have to check for proper placement of the tube and then transfer any remaining milk into a syringe. Next, we would attach it to the end of the tube coming out of his nose and raise the tube of milk into the air and let gravity carry the milk down into Caleb's stomach. This took about thirty minutes to get one ounce down into his stomach. We had to take it slow because if we gave him too much too fast he could throw up. If that happened, we would have to feed him all over again because we didn't want him to become dehydrated and run the risk of losing him. Once we were done we had to pull back on the syringe until we saw milk just to be sure all of the air was out of the stomach. As we all know no one likes a colicky baby.

The next step of the process which was the car seat test, is one that we were so looking forward to. We had heard so much about it and it was the last test to be done before we were able to take Caleb home. We were so excited! It would determine if it was safe enough to transport Caleb home. We lived about an hour and a half away from Loma Linda, CA. and in order for Caleb to pass he would have to sit in the car seat for the same amount of time it would take us to get him home. This all took place while he was monitored on the pulse-ox. If his heart rate changed or is oxygen saturations dropped that meant he wasn't ready and we would have to try again another time. We placed Caleb in the car seat and were on edge the entire duration of the observation. We were praying Caleb would pass so we could finally go home! Five minutes passed, and Caleb was doing fine. Another five minutes had passed, and Caleb was still doing fine. Then thirty minutes passed and lo and behold, Caleb was still doing great. We hit an hour and no changes! We had just a half an hour to go then we would be home free. The last thirty minutes passed and praise God our little Caleb was officially eligible to go home. We were absolutely elated that Caleb passed on the very first try!

Two and a half weeks had gone by and we had done all the training and were practically taking care of Caleb on our own now. The doctor's rounded that morning and decided Caleb was ready to go home now. I could hardly believe what I was hearing! Home? Caleb? Wow! Caleb was finally well enough to go home. They said they were confident that John and I could do it on your own now. John and I looked at each other in amazement but it was time. The doctor said I will put in all the orders for the medication and the equipment he will need. The only thing left to learn was how to use the Kangaroo pump. This pump would only be used to continuously feed Caleb milk throughout the night. Caleb was very tiny, and the doctors knew this would help him gain weight for the next surgery (Glenn) that would happen when he was six months old. The nurse came in and went over how to use the pump and thankfully it was very simple. We caught on fairly quickly, so she gathered all of our paperwork together, so we could take Caleb home.

John and I were extremely excited but also scared to death. We went over the discharge information and were handed a schedule for medication and feeds that they had been using since Caleb had been there. She filled up a bag with syringes, 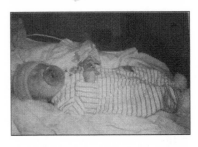 tape, ng tubes and any other supplies they thought we would need at home until our insurance company started sending them. Once the prescriptions were filled, we loaded everything into the car. As I sat there getting Caleb ready to go home I started crying. John and the nurse asked me what was wrong. It had just hit me that we were going home, and that John and I would have to do everything. I realized at that moment that if I didn't do something right, if I missed a medication, or gave him too much, or not enough I could put Caleb's life in danger. It was a major responsibility and the reality of that was now sinking in. They reassured us that it would be ok and that we could do this. Irene just happened to enter the room as I was crying and reaffirmed that we would do just fine. She also gave me her contact information in case we had any questions or issues and said to feel free to call day or night! She then instructed me to call her as soon as we made it home to let her know that we made it safely.

We loaded Caleb into the car seat and walked down the hallway. As we were leaving all of the nurses gathered at the doors and wished us well. We had made so many friends which had astonishingly somewhere along the journey became family. I was happy to go but also sad because we all had become so close. We strapped Caleb into the car and set out on our journey home. I sat in the back seat, because I wanted to keep an eye on Caleb just in case something happened on the drive home. John and I talked all the way home reassuring each other that we were a team and that we could do this. I was on the phone calling countless people to tell them that Caleb was in the car and that we were on our way home.

We arrived home, unloaded the car, and we got everything all set up. Caleb's homecoming wasn't like other families where everyone comes over to celebrate the new baby. We only allowed a few people to visit. While they were visiting I noticed the time and it was almost seven o'clock. I knew it was almost time for Caleb to eat and get his night medications. John and I got the equipment set up and double checked to make sure it was done correctly. We then performed a third check to confirm we didn't make any mistakes. Once 8pm hit we gave him his medications and set him up on the kangaroo pump for his night feeds. John hooked Caleb up to the pulse-ox and we prayed over Caleb asking the Lord to watch over him while we slept. We tried to get some sleep, but there was no way to rest, it was up to us now. It was the longest night of our lives. We both kept checking on him constantly. We just wanted to make sure we didn't miss anything, and that Caleb was ok.

Praise God we made it through the first night. The next few days were very trying and definitely took some getting used to. Caleb had a strictly regimented routine. With his medications, having to be fed every two and a half hours, plus the fact I was still pumping so that he could get all the nutrients from my breast milk left me feeling drained. Camille and I talked every day trying to reassure each other that we could do this. Irene the nurse from Loma Linda called every day to be sure we were doing everything on time and that Caleb was receiving all his medications. As much as I hated it I realized that all this was so important because if we forgot one thing it could cost Caleb his life. I wasn't getting much sleep with the routine and I felt like a zombie. I just kept telling myself in time I will adjust, and it won't be like this forever.

It was time for Caleb's follow up appointments with all of his doctors. We told them Caleb was continuing to have a hard time sucking from a bottle and was still mostly being fed through the ng tube. The doctor's checked his weight and growth very closely and were concerned that if Caleb didn't get the proper nutrition it could affect his body and his overall heart function. Being that Caleb only had half of a heart they expressed how important it was to stay on top of everything. I told them that we would be sure to do so. Caleb was having several tests performed to ensure he was up to par. He had an echocardiogram, blood pressure check, and blood draw to make sure all his levels were where they were supposed to be. This definitely wasn't the normal well baby check-up most parents have after their child is born. This was way more than that, and it was a bit much to handle especially because I was so tired. During the tests I even had to step away for a moment to go pump. I sat there thinking how wild all this was, how much life had changed and that as long as we had Caleb this was what life was going to be.

After all the tests were done it was time to talk with Dr. B. He told use Caleb was doing well and all of his tests looked great. He said I don't want to see you for two weeks. That was the best news ever. We loaded up and headed home. When we got home I bathed Caleb and put him in fresh clothes. I had learned that the doctor's offices and the hospital were full of germs and germs were our enemy. We definitely didn't want Caleb to get sick. We knew that any type of infection could hurt or even kill him. I was super paranoid and had to be sure that Caleb was germ free.

Caleb was still having trouble drinking from the bottle, but I was determined to get him to drink from it. Little by little Caleb started to get the hang of the suck, swallow, breathe technique and could finally drink from the bottle. John and I were so happy we could remove that NG tube out of his nose. Caleb was even able to take all his medications orally now. It was a very exciting day when we were able to remove the NG tube. Caleb looked so handsome without the tube on his face. I must have taken hundreds of pictures that day. I was so proud that Caleb could eat again like he did before surgery.

I was instructed to apply for Social Security to help with assistance because Caleb was going to have surgeries and medication that John's insurance wouldn't cover. We were living in my grandparent's home that my mother and other family members had inherited once my grandparents passed away. When I went to the Social Security office to turn in all the paperwork required to get Caleb qualified, I found out that I needed some type of rental agreement to complete the process. My Mother of course was willing to fill out an agreement but because others were on the deed I needed all of their signatures as well. Under any other circumstance I wasn't sure if I would be able to obtain the other family members signatures, but since it was for Caleb I didn't think there would be an issue. Boy, was I wrong! I reached out to one and at first, they were going to cooperate until they found out another family member was unwilling, so they changed their mind. I couldn't believe this was actually happening. I was so hurt and couldn't understand why they would do this. I tried talking with one of them trying to understand why. All they kept saying was something about taxes and that they weren't going to put themselves in any kind of trouble with the IRS. I was so hurt, I lashed out and said "OK! But if I can't get Caleb all the things he needs, and he dies his blood will be on your hands!" I hung up the phone devastated, and in disbelief that this was happening. I cried and felt so betrayed that my heart broke into a thousand pieces for my son. I couldn't fathom that they weren't even willing to look out for him! This was horrible!

I went back to the SSI office embarrassed and had to explain what had happened. I hoped they would tell me there was another way I could get what they needed without the signatures from those family members. The worker instructed me go to a local rental place and ask them to find a home like my Grandparent's and find out how much they would rent it for. Have them put the details on their company letterhead and bring it back to them.

I left immediately and went to the nearest realty company. I asked them if they could help me. I was embarrassed, but I had to do this for Caleb. I explained what was going on and of course they were willing to help. The agent said unfortunately there is a small fee that I can't wave. I said that was ok the fee is not an issue. I was just happy that there was a way around the situation. They found a property similar to my grandparent's home and I explained the SSI office needed the quote to be on their letterhead to show it was official. They got the statement ready right away and I was able to turn it in that same day. What a relief, in spite of what my family had tried to do I was able to initiate the process and Caleb qualified for SSI. I was still a little upset about the entire ordeal, but thankfully the process was underway.

It took some time but paperwork from the Social Security office started coming. I finally received the letter that Caleb did indeed qualify. John made too much money where he worked but thankfully Caleb was able to receive medical benefits. I was informed that because Caleb was disabled he also qualified for Home Supportive Services. I went to their office and filled out all the paperwork. Once Caleb was enrolled, the next step was to wait for a representative to come and perform an assessment to determine the hours they would authorize. I couldn't understand why there was so much paperwork to be done just to make sure Caleb had what he needed. It made no sense to me, the only thing I should have to focus on was taking care of my son who had a very serious illness which the doctors had classified as "terminal".

A few weeks later the social worker and nurse from IHSS would come and assessed Caleb. There was so much paperwork to go over and sign. The social worker went over all the rules and explained how the program was set up. I was told I had to attend a class to learn more about the program and that's where I would learn how to fill out my timesheet. I thought, what a great program that would enable me to stay home and care for my child. She told me when the next available date was and explained I needed to attend. Without that class being completed I couldn't fill out my time sheet and received any benefits.

As the social worker was leaving the nurse was arriving. It was her turn to assess Caleb. She asked me tons of questions about Caleb's daily routine. We went over every possible detail. I got Caleb's charts and showed her his very busy schedule. The nurse was amazed, she didn't know how I kept up with all of it. I told her it wasn't easy but somehow, we made it work. The nurse proceeded to look Caleb over. She noticed Caleb had a bluish gray tinge to his skin. I explained Caleb's defect to her, so she could understand a little better. She was amazed that Caleb was doing as well as he was despite his circumstances and kept repeating how adorable Caleb was. I had to agree Caleb was a very handsome little fella.

Caleb was doing great and life seemed to be getting a little easier. It was hard to believe Caleb was two months old now. I went down to Loma Linda mistakenly thinking Caleb had a doctor's appointment. I told the nurse practitioner that I had noticed Caleb's hands and feet were a little bluer than they had been in the past. Dr. B said since I was already there to go ahead and do an echo just to be on the safe side. Caleb and I went upstairs, and they performed the echo. After they were done the technician told me to go back down to the doctor's office and the doctor would be there shortly to discuss with me what the echo showed. I thought this was strange and started to get a little concerned because usually after the echo we would just go home. Dr. R, Caleb's surgeon, came into the room where we were waiting and told me that the echo revealed Caleb's aorta had narrowed. I was in shock and I started shaking and began to cry. He explained that we would not be leaving. Caleb needed to be monitored closely because what they had found was life threatening. He explained that Caleb would need to have surgery in the morning. I couldn't believe what I was hearing. Caleb was doing so well and now to find out the reason his hands and feet were bluer was because his aorta had narrowed! This couldn't be happening!

I called John immediately and told him what the doctor said. I was trying keep my composure while I was talking to John, but all the while I was falling apart on the inside. John couldn't believe what I was telling him either. He was at work, so he informed his supervisor and told me he would be on his way. We hung up the phone and I knew he was rushing trying to get to us. He had to go home and pack a bag for us then drive to Loma Linda. I was so worried about him, I knew he would be driving fast and with all this on his mind I started praying for his safe travels.

I had to wait in the clinic until they could get a bed ready for Caleb in the CVICU. I was holding Caleb so tight. I was afraid to put him down because deep down inside that overwhelming feeling had come back again that I was going to lose my baby. We weren't supposed to have another surgery until Caleb was six months old. The nurses and doctors were so kind, they kept checking on us and asking me if I was ok. They asked if I wanted to lay Caleb down or if I wanted them to help me, but I just couldn't let him go I was too afraid.

John finally got there. I was so relieved to see him. He grabbed Caleb from me and held him tightly. John began to shower Caleb with kisses and telling him how much he loved him. Shortly after John's arrival Caleb's room was ready. We carried him to the room and settled in for the night. I was holding Caleb in the rocking chair singing to him Jesus loves the little children. I just kept hoping that this was all a nightmare and that I would wake up soon, but it was really happening. Neither one of us could believe this was happening to Caleb and that he was headed for another surgery in only a few short hours. John and I stayed bedside because we were in disbelief and didn't want to leave Caleb.

That night was very long night. We couldn't stop thinking of all the different scenarios. There were doctors in and out all-night checking on Caleb and explaining the procedure. They went over the benefits and risks and some of what they said was hard to accept. Who wants to hear that their child could possibly bleed to death and die during the procedure? Dr. B explained it was the best way to determine if he could balloon the aorta open. He told us that the procedure was called a heart catheterization and that this was the easiest way to access the area without having to reopen Caleb and do another open-heart surgery. He told us they would be making small incisions in his neck and leg where he would insert the catheter with the balloon on the end. He would use ultrasound and make his way through his arteries until he reached the part of the aorta that had narrowed. Once there he would inflate and deflate the balloon attempting to reopen the aorta but if he was unsuccessful he might have to insert a stent. He then added if none of that worked, Caleb would have to have another open-heart surgery. There was no way his aorta could be left like that because it was Caleb's main blood supply. Now we understood why everyone is so concerned about Caleb. Dr. B pulled out the paperwork and asked for one of us to sign and to give them authorization to do the procedure. I just couldn't bring myself to do it, so John provided the signature.

It was time to walk Caleb to the Cath lab. As we headed to the elevator my whole body felt like Jell-O. I don't even know how I was able to stand, let alone walk. We entered that small brightly lit place again. John hit the button and we were going down. I was staring at the floor attempting to fight back tears. I wanted to scream because I couldn't understand why this was happening to my sweet baby boy. The doors opened, and we started to walk to the Cath lab, all the while John had a firm grasp on my hand. We reached the door where we couldn't go any further, so we whispered a prayer over Caleb and the entire team that would be working on him. John and I took turns kissing Caleb then it was time for him to go back. Again, all we could do is stand there and watch Caleb go. The hardest part was the uncertainty if it would be the last time we saw him alive. I looked up to heaven and once again asked God to have mercy on my beautiful baby boy.

We were instructed to go to the waiting room and told as soon as they were done the doctor would come talk to us. We didn't talk much as we waited. Really, what was there to talk about? We didn't want to express what was really going on in our minds, so we just sat there watching the people around us. We got one update telling us Caleb was doing great and that he was stable. That was a little relief, but I knew I wouldn't feel better until Caleb was safe in my arms. The procedure took about two hours and then Dr. B came to talk to us. He explained that it went very well and that he was able to balloon his aorta open. Oh my, we were so excited! It worked, and Caleb didn't have to have another open-heart surgery. Thank God! I asked Dr. B if I could give him a hug and he agreed! I was so thankful he saved Caleb. Dr. B told us Caleb would have to stay another night for observation and that in the morning Caleb would have another echo to make sure the aorta remained open. Dr. B said Caleb was on his way back to the room and that by the time we got up to the fifth floor we should be able to see him.

We were enthused to get this news and of course John and I started calling everyone to let them know Caleb was ok. What a relief Caleb was out of danger! I began thanking God for hearing our prayers and allowing Caleb to stay with us. Tears of happiness rolled down our faces as John and I hugged one another, so grateful that our baby had survived something so serious. We were elated that we'd be able to hold our baby soon. We couldn't get up to the CVICU fast enough, so we could see Caleb's handsome little face. The receptionist called back, and the nurse said send them in. We entered and there was our precious little boy. He was resting so we didn't want to bother him. We whispered a prayer to God thanking Him again for all he had done for Caleb. It was almost shift change, so we headed out asking the nurse to please call us if anything changed.

During shift change John and I went to go have a nice dinner and celebrate. John took me to my favorite place to eat, Red Lobster. At dinner the conversation was minimal because we both were exhausted from all the day's festivities. What a roller coaster we had been on in less than twenty-four hours. We went from doing a simple echo to finding out Caleb's aorta had narrowed, to having an emergency surgery to reopen it. What a day but thank God Dr. B was able to reopen it and Caleb was doing well. We finished dinner and headed back to the hospital. Caleb was awake and a little fussy. The nurse explained Caleb was sore from the surgery and that the doctor had ordered Tylenol. She said that would help him and added that she had just got the ok for Caleb to start feeds. I happily sat down in the rocking chair and the nurse handed me Caleb. She said Caleb could only have an ounce because they wanted to be sure after all the anesthesia he could tolerate eating. It felt so great to have Caleb in my arms once again. Needless to say, the tears started, and emotions overcame me as before. I was so thankful to be able to hold such a precious gift how could I not cry.

John and I stayed right by Caleb's side through the night. We knew there was a chance that his aorta could narrow again and that we'd be right back in the same situation, but this time Caleb would have to be opened for the repair. We tried to rest but there was so much traffic from doctors coming by to make sure Caleb's was doing well. The morning came quickly, and the technician came bright and early to get the echo done. All the doctors were concerned and the only way to be certain was with the echo. Dr. B didn't want to wait to see the reports, so he sat there with the technician and watched as she performed the echocardiogram. As she scanned all the areas of Caleb's heart everything looked great. Dr. B was giving us all the details and pointing out the different things she was taking pictures of so that we would have a better understanding of Caleb's anatomy. The moment of truth had arrived, and my heart started pounding as she positioned Caleb's body so that she could see Caleb's aorta clearly. All eyes were glued to the monitor and although John and I had no idea what we were looking at, we knew they did. She scanned and measured the flow of blood through his aorta. They both started to smile, and Dr. B told us with great excitement Caleb's aorta stayed open and looks amazing!

Dr. B was very pleased with all he saw on the echo and because he was happy we were as well. He told us he would have our discharge paperwork done shortly and we could take Caleb home. That was the news we were waiting for. Of course, before

Dr. B left I hugged him as usual, I was so thankful for all he had done for Caleb. John and I got Caleb dressed and prepared to go home. We hugged and kissed him repeatedly whereas we were so thankful to the Lord for keeping Caleb safe. The nurse came in very quickly and we were able to leave. We walked down the hall and all the nurses waved goodbye. Going home we came to realize was the goal for all the children and we were more than happy to do so. Right at that moment it hit me, but what about these babies who can't! My heart began to hurt for them and their parents. How could I be so happy for my family when other families were still there facing the reality that they may never go home. I cried out to God and asked Him to please give them strength and comfort. I knew then that somehow, I wanted to help them all on their journey.

We were glad to be back home. John and I reflected on all that we had been through as we bathed Caleb and got all the possible germs off him. I told John about how I'd felt for the other families as we were leaving. I explained how my heart broke and the feelings of guilt that our baby was well enough to leave but theirs weren't. I told John I wanted to help them in some way. I wasn't exactly sure how, but I was definitely going to figure something out. Afterwards we all settled in and got some much-needed rest.

The next few months we had the process down. Caleb's routine consisted of daily calls from Irene, doctors' appointments, and making sure Caleb was eating so he could gain weight. At one of the appointments they performed an echocardiogram as usual. After it was over we headed to clinic to discuss the results with Dr. B. We were in the room waiting and Dr. B came in and delivered the news that the echo revealed that all of Caleb's arteries were narrowing. He said it was very concerning because everywhere Dr. R had put a patch was narrowing and making it harder for Caleb's heart to pump the blood. He told us as we had discussed before that most children go in for the Glenn at six months, but Caleb would have to be scheduled as soon as possible. My heart dropped! I felt like I was going to throw up. My heart was racing because we had just learned Caleb wasn't doing well at all. He was once again in danger. We couldn't believe what we were hearing. Just knowing that Caleb would be having his second open-heart surgery caused me to cry uncontrollably. I handed Caleb to John and broke down. Dr. B said he was sorry but unfortunately this was what they had discovered and in order to help Caleb there was no other option.

I asked if he wanted to check Caleb in, so we could get it done right away. He said that we could take him home and that he had already placed a call in to Dr. R to work out the details. I was devastated. Although we were allowed to take him home, Dr. B said that he wanted to intervene before anything else got worse. My mind was blown as to how I was going to be able to function knowing that all of Caleb's arteries were narrowing and his heart had to work much harder to pump blood to his organs. Just when we thought that things couldn't have gotten any worse we were now receiving what was possibly the worse news imaginable. I was a wreck but desperately trying to hold it together. The car ride home was quite apart from the sobbing as we both shed tears. I silently asked God how this could be happening! My heart was broken, and my precious baby was having to endure such difficult circumstances.

Caleb had to have multiple tests conducted before he could be scheduled for surgery. We made repeated trips back and forth to Loma Linda in preparation for the surgery. Once all of the tests were completed we were finally given the surgery date of February 16, 2007. Ok, I remember thinking! There is no choice at this point. Living life wasn't easy because I knew what was happening inside of Caleb. At least once the surgery was done and everything was corrected he'd be out of danger and maybe then we could get back to some kind of normalcy! John worked the graveyard shift so when I got the call I didn't want to bother him with that news until he woke up. At least he would be able to rest now.

February 16th came quickly, and we went down the night before because Caleb was the first case. Dr. R was unsure how long it would take him to do the repairs on the patches and he also had to do the Glenn where he would move the superior vena cava over to the pulmonary artery. We had to be at the hospital by 5 am so we tried to lay down early and rest. I didn't get much sleep that night, I knew Caleb had a major operation coming. I prayed earnestly for all the staff that God would guide their minds and hands to do exactly what God's will was for Caleb. I was very frightened and so many thoughts were racing through my mind. I was trying to be positive, but I knew Caleb had a long road ahead of him.

The staff once again surrounded the bed and it was time to go. At this point I felt completely numb, it felt as if my body was literally shutting down. At the elevator again and I was in such a daze that I don't even recall who hit the button. We all entered the elevator and headed down to the surgery ward. The elevator opened and there we were again at the doors where they prepared that special place for Caleb's surgery. My heart sank as I tried holding back the tears. I was trembling and terrified for Caleb, but I knew there was no other choice. It would seem that this time around it would be easier but that was far from the case. John and I whispered a word of prayer for Caleb prayed once again for God to orchestrate the entire procedure. We kissed him and let him know that we loved him as they wheeled Caleb through the doors. We stood in shock as the doors close. It was getting harder and harder each time to let him go. The only thing we could do was to put our faith in God that His perfect will would be done.

As we headed up the elevator the horrible feeling of dread came over me. All the thoughts of what the doctors had told us prior to Caleb going in hit me. I was thinking of all the worst-case scenarios that could happen during surgery. I began to cry out to the Lord that He wouldn't let any of those things happen. I began to weep as I begged the Lord to have mercy on Caleb and to bring him back to me safely. I knew I was being selfish, but I loved him so much. I knew life without him would be unbearable. Caleb had claimed my heart and life without him would be so empty.

As we headed to the waiting room I couldn't stop crying. John was such a huge support reassuring me everything would be ok. Hours passed as we waited and waited. We knew it was a sign that there had to be something wrong. Although we received a few updates, we still weren't clear on exactly what was going on. We walked back and forth pacing the floor and it seemed like we went up and down that hallway a thousand times. Finally, the call came that Caleb would be up from surgery in about thirty minutes and that the doctor would be in soon to go over the details. What a relief to know that Caleb made it through surgery. In the midst of all of the uncertainty, our joy soon turned into fear when thirty minutes came and went and there was still no sign of the Dr. R or Caleb. Once again, I was faced with the possibilities of what could be happening or had gone wrong. Every time the elevator doors opened we just knew it would be Caleb, but it wasn't. John and I began to panic, we just knew something had went wrong. We asked the receptionist, but she didn't have any answers for us. Up and down the hall we continued to pace and finally after what seemed like an eternity in hell, the elevator doors opened, and the doctor and Caleb appeared. My heart melted when I laid eyes on them. My baby! He was still here praise God! While passing by, Dr. R told us that once he got Caleb settled he'd be out to talk to us. We went in the room and waited. John and I didn't talk much. The tension in the air was thick because we had no idea what to expect. After about forty-five minutes the doctor came in to talk to us. Dr. R explained that Caleb's scarring was extensive and unlike anything he had ever seen in all the years he had been performing this particular surgery. He went on to tell us that every place that he had patched in the first surgery was attacked by Caleb's body and had scarred. Caleb's body was rejecting the cadaver tissue and that was the reason the surgery took so long.

It turns out that Dr. R had to do the first surgery all over again and then perform the second surgery called the Glen. This procedure entails detaching the superior vena cava from the atrium and re-attaching it to the pulmonary artery. Dr. R explained that Caleb was a very sick little boy and the next 48 hours would determine what would happen. This was the worst news ever. I broke down and all I could do was cry and pray. I knew however that I needed to get myself together because I wanted to be able to see my son. I knew Caleb's vessels had narrowed but I was unaware that it was to this extent. Dr. R's words kept ringing in my head over and over that Caleb was a very sick little boy and the next 48 hours would determine what would happen to him.

The nurses were done and now it was time to see Caleb. I was frightened as we entered the room. He was connected to an unbelievable amount of tubes that were all supplying medications to help keep him alive. Caleb was intubated so I was unable to hold him. It was absolutely heartbreaking to see Caleb like this. We were back to the scheduled visits of 15 minutes once per hour. With the next 48 hours being so critical we knew that it would be difficult to consistently make the visits? Fifteen minutes was nothing. He would need his rest, but I wanted to be by his side every single minute of every single hour.

We went to see Caleb a few times that evening. John and I were exhausted from the roller coaster of emotions, so we decided to try and get some rest. We whispered a word of prayer over Caleb and as we were leaving asked the nurse to contact us if anything changed with Caleb. We arrived back at the Ronald McDonald house, but we didn't get much sleep that night because we were nervous about what the next 48 hours were going to bring. How could any parent rest knowing that their child is critically ill and literally fighting for their life?

We were up bright and early to go see Caleb. We walked into the room and to our surprise there were electrodes connected all over his little head. John and I were shocked because we had no idea what was going on. Once the nurse saw the expression on our faces, she began to explain that they had seen some involuntary movements in Caleb's face and hand which could mean seizure activity. We were very upset that we hadn't been notified. The last words we told the nurse when we left was if ANYTHING changed to call us immediately! We were completely unprepared for this and began to once again wrestle internally. Was Caleb really having seizures?

He was connected to an EEG (Electroencephalography) machine which records brain activity and would indicate if Caleb was indeed having seizures. John and I were upset and scared. We asked to see the doctor's immediately, so we  could find out exactly what was going on. Dr. R and Dr. B came in and gave us the news that Caleb had been having nonstop seizures for the last 24 hours. Dr. B explained that he may have to rush Caleb into the Cath lab to close the shunt off. What? Did he just say rush Caleb into the Cath lab? At that point I went numb. The next words he said made me lose it! Dr. B said it was possibly too much for his body to handle and could be causing Caleb's brain damage. You mean to tell me that the shunt could possibly be causing him to have the seizures. I almost fell down. We were just blindsided by all of this. We woke up thinking Caleb had a restful night, but it was not the case at all. I had to sit down and get myself together. Brain damage? Another surgery? Was all this really happening?

Dr. R chimed in and told us he had started Caleb on anti-seizure medication in hopes of stopping the seizures. If the medication worked and got them under control Caleb could possibly avoid another surgery. We started praying immediately for Caleb that he would respond to the medication and that the seizures would stop. We could only stay fifteen minutes and had to leave but I was not ready to. I wanted to stay with Caleb, he was going through so much and I wanted to be right there by his side. Who was I kidding, what I wanted really didn't matter, I had no choice, I had to leave. As a precaution, I made sure that the nurse and all of the staff was very clear that if there were ANY changes in Caleb that we were to be notified immediately! I made sure that everyone had both of our numbers written down. Walking out of the room I looked over my shoulder wishing I could take all of this away for my baby boy. We were so ready to be awakened from this nightmare.

As we were leaving Dr. R told us that he had contacted a neurologist to come and evaluate Caleb. He wanted to get things started right away to help treat Caleb. John and I arrived at the elevators and looked at one another is disbelief. I started weeping and all John could do was hold me. I knew he couldn't even tell me everything was going to be ok because he wasn't even sure himself. We went to the cafeteria and tried to get something to eat but I soon realized that I wasn't even hungry. John reminded me I needed to keep my strength up for Caleb. Although I had no appetite, I forced myself to get a little food down to ensure that I would have adequate milk supply when pumping for Caleb.

An hour had passed, and it was finally time to go see Caleb again. We entered the room and were told that Caleb's whole left side was not working but that he had responded to the medication. He wasn't having any more seizures. Wow! That was great news, but the other portion was devastating! Clearly it had to have been something much more serious than the seizures for the left side of his body not to be working. I went over to grasp Caleb's left hand and it was lifeless. I tried to hold back, but the tears just kept falling! My poor son, how could all this be happening? He was only four months old!

We were given the pleasure of meeting Dr. A. He was the Neurologist taking care of Caleb. He told us the extent of the damage to his brain and explained that even though it was extensive, Caleb was young enough to recover. He told us that his brain could reprogram itself and with assistance he would be just fine. That was good news, but it still didn't change Caleb's current situation. Dr. A said he would monitor Caleb very closely and order therapy for him. It was hard enough to deal with Caleb having his second open-heart surgery but now a stroke that could affect him for this for the rest of his life. This was just simply too much, and I had to get out of there. I walked out of the room shaking badly. I had no idea where I was going but I had to get out of there before I lost it. John followed me. He tried talking, but there was nothing that he could he say at that point that would lighten the weight of what we'd just heard. As I sobbed John held me although I knew he was feeling helpless as well.

At the Ronald McDonald house I met the sweetest young mother who had a little girl. That night over dinner she explained to us all about her daughter being born premature and only weighing 1 lb. 7 oz. She told us the NICU doctors had over fed her and destroyed her small intestines and now she needed an intestinal transplant. The baby was unable to eat anything by mouth, so she had to be fed intravenously with TPN (Total Parenteral Nutrition). TNP was great and helped keep the little girl alive but she was concerned because she knew it would eventually hurt her liver. TPN has high fat content which could cause her liver to fail. What a sad story! I felt bad for her. It was so nice having someone there during such a crazy period. We exchanged numbers, so we could keep in contact.

It finally came time to take Caleb home. During that visit Caleb was on so many narcotics that his little body was detoxing extremely bad. His body was so sensitive that he couldn't be touched or moved because it would make him throw up. Even something as simple as touching him caused pain to the point of making him cry. It was absolutely heartbreaking not to be able to hold and love on my baby. I didn't want to hurt him even more, so we limited touching him. The only thing we could do to comfort him was to pat his tummy. Although my poor little guy had been through so much in such a short time, Caleb was still here fighting with all that he had, and we were determined to do the same.

John and I realized quickly just how sick Caleb really was. We got specialist involved to help us with Caleb's recovery. Slowly but surely Caleb began to get better. From all of the trauma Caleb's body had been through he couldn't suck from a bottle and had to be tube fed. I made Caleb an appointment with a feeding specialist hoping to get help and get some training on how to get Caleb to feed without the assistance of the NG tube. That's when I was introduced to thick-it. Thick-it is a food and beverage thickener that can be added to foods or beverages to thicken them and help the individual not choke when eating.

The specialist was concerned about Caleb aspirating every time he swallowed thin fluids, so she decided to order a barium swallow test. This test would indicate exactly how much Caleb was aspirating when he swallowed and assist in determining how to get him fixed and eating again. The results were high, so she referred us to an ENT doctor for further guidance on what needed to take place. I called and made the appointment right away.

In the meantime, I started adding the thick-it to Caleb's milk. He slowly started getting the hang of swallowing. As he got better with the consistency, I slowly decreased the amount of thick-it I added to his milk and eventually he was able to drink from a cup without choking. I was elated that my little guy was doing so well and getting stronger by the day. Things were finally getting back to as normal as they could be with a child who had only half a heart.

We got all of Caleb's services set up with IRC (Inland Regional Center). They sent out a wonderful woman named Theresa. She visited once a week and worked with us all on how to strengthen Caleb's body. We had to work with him extensively, especially his left side because of how it was affected by the stroke. Every day I worked with Caleb's hand, arm, and leg and they slowly started to work again. He was regaining his strength and we were so proud of our little Caleb. He was even reaching for things and able to hold his own cup.

Caleb had an appointment where he was scheduled to receive the flu shot. We were uncertain if we wanted it to be administered but the doctors were so adamant about him receiving it. They alluded to the fact that he needed every bit of protection that he could possibly get so we eventually conceded. Afterwards, I had noticed when he was taking a nap he was breathing a little strange but didn't really think too much of it because his stats were good. Theresa came over and was working with Caleb and he started holding his breath. Caleb at times would get upset and could hold his breath for almost a minute during a tantrum. When he would have one I'd have to walk him around to take his mind off everything, so he'd start back breathing. I thought at that moment that's what Caleb was doing. I decided to take him outside because that normally seemed to work. Once we were outside Caleb went limp. Theresa grabbed him and took him back in the house and laid him on the floor. She started to perform CPR as I called 911. My heart was racing while I was on the phone. I couldn't believe this was happening. Thank God the ambulance arrived very quickly. They gave Caleb a shot to open his airways and he started breathing again. Because of Caleb's history they took us to the hospital. They were on the phone with Loma Linda immediately. They all decided it would be in Caleb's best interest to get to Loma Linda as fast as possible, so they sent a helicopter to pick Caleb up. We couldn't believe all this was happening. He seemed to be doing so well and making a substantial amount of progress but was now being loaded into a helicopter heading back to Loma Linda. John and I couldn't get there fast enough. His breathing episode had us wondering if our baby would actually be able to pull through.

Once we arrived we rushed up to the CVICU. They led us back right away and there in the room was our sweet little boy doing awesome! His numbers looked good and he was awake smiling. Tears of joy ran down my face and his smiling face was the best sight in the world. I was grateful enough that he was alive but for him to be smiling was the icing on the cake! Praise God for once again watching over Caleb.

The doctors came in and that's when we found out that Caleb was allergic to the flu shot. Dr. B said no more shots for Caleb. We definitely didn't want that to happen again. We all breathed a big sigh of relief and said, "That's for sure". Dr. B told us I'm keeping him over night but tomorrow if everything goes well you can take Caleb back home. Everything went well throughout the night and sure enough we were able to take Caleb home and try to get back to our new normal.

Meanwhile, life was still going on. All of my time was devoted to Caleb, making it difficult to give attention the other people in my life. My daughter Ashley and niece Erica were in high school with their own struggles and then to add Caleb to all of this was just a bit much for everyone. John and I were still struggling to adjust to the sudden changes and it was definitely placing a strain on our marriage. Like I said, all of my attention was on Caleb, so we were losing sight of one another. It is hard to have a normal life when you have a child that needs around the clock care. We were all trying to move on as best as we could but the reality that Caleb could leave us at any moment was a difficult thing to overlook. I decided to go back to school and at least finish my AS. I chose to do it all on-line, so that I could be at home with Caleb. Besides, with all that Caleb required, how was I going to be able to attend school?

Caleb was doing awesome and now it was time to close the shunt that was inserted at the second open-heart surgery. Dr. K would be the doctor that would be performing the surgery. We checked Caleb into the hospital early that morning. Of course, Caleb was the first case. They wanted to allow adequate time just in case they ran into anything unexpected once they were in Caleb's arteries. Here we go again. It was so hard for Caleb and us both to have to continuously go through this over and over. Although some say that they can relate to our pain, I truly believe that unless one has been in the same situation that they can never truly comprehend what it feels like.

Once in the cath lab the doctor saw that his left pulmonary had narrowed again and there was only a small amount of blood flowing into his left lung. Dr. K came out and spoke with us. He said, "I hate to tell you this, but Caleb's body did it again. There is a tiny bit of blood getting through, but the opening is so small that I couldn't get the catheter through." Dr. K told us that he had a colleague at Randy's Children's hospital in San Diego that may be able to help. He explained that if anyone could get Caleb's left pulmonary artery open it would be him.

Caleb's surgery just happened to be in February and that's when Loma Linda does a big event for heart awareness. February (which most people don't know) is heart awareness month. Ironically, Camille was there at the same time with Lauren. We decided to take a little break and go to the lobby to see what was going on. There were booths set up everywhere with different organizations. They were there letting people know what resources they offered and how they could assist the families. God had already been speaking to my spirit about helping others on their journey through life with a child who has special needs. While we were in the lobby it hit me, I knew just what I was going to do! They were handing out goody bags with markers, crayons, and coloring books. I thought that's not what these families need, they need gas and food cards. They need lodging because more times than not the Ronald McDonald house is full which leads to trying to find a place to rest. I thought of how many times these families had no choice but to sleep in their car because they were far from home and have no place to lay their head. If you've ever slept in a car before, you know you don't get much rest. So that was it, my organization would help with gas and food cards. We would also assist with lodging and any other necessities a family may have to help lessen the load during their journey.

I started praying God what do You want me to call the organization? I knew it would be helping families with very special children. The ones God hand created. The ones He uniquely designed as a special gift here on Earth. I kept saying Babies.... Babies.... Babies... Then it came to me Babies So Special. Wow! Praise God had given me the name. I told  Camille and she loved it! We said ok and just went for it. It may seem crazy but that's was how Babies So Special began. (www.babiessospecial.org)

An appointment was made for Caleb's heart cath to see if Dr. M could get Caleb's pulmonary artery open. We headed up to San Diego the day before, so they could evaluate Caleb and prepare him for surgery. The doctors thoroughly examined him and gave the green light to proceed. We finished up with the prerequisites for the surgery and then headed over to the Ronald McDonald house. After checking in, we took Caleb to the beach and had a great day. We concluded the evening with a nice dinner and headed back to the Ronald McDonald house to get some rest. We had no idea what the next day was going to bring, considering all of the curve balls we had been thrown in the past.

We arrived for Caleb's appointment bright and early in the morning. Caleb's condition was so unpredictable that every doctor wanted plenty of time just in case they ran into something they had not anticipated. They prepped Caleb for his procedure and Dr. M came in and spoke with us on what his plans were. Shortly after our discussion, the staff emerged, and they wheeled Caleb away. As they were leaving, we once again prayed God's blessings over him. It was a hard pill to swallow that although they initially said that he would only have three surgeries, our baby was headed off to his fifth. This was nothing like they said that it would be.

After some time had passed we got an update that Caleb was stable and doing great. The nurse told us that the procedure was almost done, and Caleb would be out soon. That was great news! About thirty minutes later Dr. M came in to talk to us. He explained that unfortunately he was unable to get through the left pulmonary artery. It was definitely not the news that we were expecting to hear. He then went on to say that while he was in there he discovered that Caleb's superior vena cava had narrowed. Dr. M explained that the reason why Caleb's face was so fat was because of the narrowing and that all of the blood was back flowing into his head. The doctor explained how dangerous it was and that we were fortunate because Caleb could have suffered a stroke at any time. Dr. M went on to explain that he had a colleague named Dr. H at Lucile Packard Children's hospital in Palo Alto, CA. He told us that Dr. H specialized in pulmonary issues and that he was the best. He asked if he could send him Caleb's case and see if he would help. Of course, we agreed whereas we were willing to do anything to help Caleb. Although we were thankful for another opportunity to help our son, we were still left with a list of questions. How did we even get here? Why did all these different things keep happening to Caleb? Where was God at in all of this? When was he going to heal Caleb and allow him to live the life he deserved? In spite of all the questions, we knew that God was in control and that through this we were learning to be more dependent upon Him.

During our time at Rady's I received a call from that young mother. I was so happy to hear from her. She asked me how Caleb was doing as we both apologized for not keeping in better touch. I asked how her little girl was and that's when she began to tell me the story. She explained that her daughter was doing great at the hospital but because of all the time she had been on TNP it had destroyed her daughter's liver. Not only did she need an intestinal transplant, she also needed a liver transplant. She had to be transferred to another hospital for the transplant and got a bladder infection while waiting. She couldn't take anything orally, so they had to inject the medication to treat the infection straight into her bladder. The time finally came, and she was transferred to the other hospital to await her transplant. I listened enthusiastically to the story, all the while thinking praise God she's about to tell me the best news ever. That was so far from the truth. She went on to say that one day she was exhausted and went home to get some rest and clean clothes. I knew that feeling all too well being at the hospital constantly. No breaks, psychosis from listening to beeping machines, trying to keep up the pace of being in the hospital. She had gone to sleep and got a phone call in the middle of the night from the hospital. They had made a grave mistake and she needed to get back right away. They rushed back to the hospital as fast as they could and once there the doctor explained what the mistake was. Unfortunately, the doctor had mistakenly wrote the order for the bladder medication for an excessive amount. The nurse had followed the orders and punctured a hole in her bladder. The doctor went on to explain that there were three things that could be done. The young mother was sad but hopeful! She asked what they were going to do to fix her baby. The doctor sadly told her that it was impossible because if they were to do anything she would bleed to death. She was then told that she would have to choose between three alternate ways of allowing her child to die! What? I couldn't believe what she had just told me! Did I hear her correctly? I sat silently in disbelief as she continued her story.

I was floored to hear this! I held back the floodgate of tears and kept apologizing that I wasn't there to help her through such a difficult time. The young mother then informed me that she wasn't finished and that there was more to the story. I said more? She said yes, I decided which way I thought was best for my precious little girl to leave this world, which was the removal of the medication. The doctor's said it would only take about an hour for her to transition from this life once the medication that supported her was decreased and that her body would simply shut down. The young mother then went on to explain that it wasn't what happened at all. Her little girl fought for an excruciating four hour until her body finally gave out and she went on to be with the Lord. My heart was so broken for her. I still couldn't believe what I was hearing. I could only imagine the devastation that she was experiencing as she went through such a horrific ordeal. That was my worst nightmare and my friend was living it!

The story only got worse as the young mother went on to tell me that she didn't have the money to bury her sweet little angel. They did some fundraising around their area such as bake sales and carwashes trying to raise the funds needed for the funeral. In spite of all of their efforts they just weren't able to raise all of the necessary funds. They went to the funeral home to give them all that they had and explained that they would get the rest to them as soon as they could raise it. The funeral home told them that if they didn't have all of the money to them before the service was scheduled that there would be no funeral. What? I was in shock, I said you're kidding me, right? The young mother sobbing said I wish I was, but I am not kidding. My heart broke for her not only did she lose her baby girl but to be treated in that manner was horrendous. At this point I wasn't sure what to say and kept apologizing to her. I felt so bad that I wasn't there to help her! I told her as soon as Caleb was home I'd be over to see her. We concluded the conversation and after the call ended I sat quietly, pondering how much better things could be if there was a support system set up for those dealing with such tragic events.

At that moment I was more determined than ever to get Babies So Special in order. I vowed that I would never let another parent beg for the money needed to lay their child to rest. As long as I have breath I will fight to make a difference in these families lives! I also decided that no matter what the child's disability is, Babies So Special would assist in any way we could.

I had to get myself back together, Caleb was still in the hospital fighting his own battle. I went back into the room feeling guilty that Caleb was still here while that young mother now had to face life without her daughter. All I could do was look at Caleb and reflect on how precious every moment was. John asked how they were doing and that's when I told him the entire story. He responded similarly to how I had and expressed his condolences for the family. It was such a horrible tragedy and a nightmare that no one should ever have to go through.

Once we got home I was on a mission. I raised as much money as I could and took it over to the young mother to use for whatever she needed it for. As soon as we saw each other we started to cry and hugged one another tightly. Our hearts were broken as we realized we were like family. This journey had brought us together and I could genuinely feel her pain. I gave her the money and she said it couldn't have come at a better time. She really needed it because when her baby had passed there was money in her account from SSI but once they were notified of the passing they took all of the money out of her account. This poor mother! She was going through possibly one of the most difficult times in her life and all I could do was to offer her a few dollars and a listening ear. I so wished I could do more, but the reality was I couldn't. I knew I needed to grow Babies So Special so big that when things like this happen we would be ready and able to assist.

A few weeks passed, and we received a call from Dr. M. He was so happy to tell us that Dr. H accepted Caleb's case and that he was willing to see if he could help. Dr. M gave me all the contact numbers and told me they were expecting my call. As soon as we hung up I called and made arrangements to travel to Northern California for Caleb's next open-heart surgery. John and I discussed how it may put a strain on things for him at work but that we would find a way to make it happen. Northern California for the next open-heart surgery! All I could think of was Ashley and how I'd have to be away from home and how she would have to be on her own. I felt so torn between my children, so I sat down and talked it over with her. She was only 16 and would now have the responsibility of handling things at home while John and I were away with Caleb. My niece Erica was also living with us and she was 17. I was concerned with leaving two teenagers at home alone, but we had no other choice whereas this may be the only hope for our precious Caleb.

It was October and we were preparing for Caleb's first birthday. Can you believe it, after all we had been through we were actually planning Caleb's first birthday party? That was a miracle in and of itself! For the celebration we would be taking out all of the stops. We realized how precious every moment was and that Caleb's birthday had to be absolutely amazing. We decided to do a farm theme and I ordered Caleb a horse costume. I was so excited and couldn't wait to put it on him. We invited all our friends and family as we looked forward to shifting our focus from everything that we had been through to simply enjoying the moment that we were in.

The day arrived, and the decorations were in place and we were so ready to get things started. We went to the local pizzeria. Everyone started arriving and it was so nice to see us all come together and celebrate Caleb's birthday. The kids played and enjoyed themselves. It was time to sing happy birthday to Caleb and he was elated when we presented him with his very own chocolate cake. Everyone gathered around and began to sing. Caleb was looking around at everyone with the biggest smile. Once they were done we blew out the candle. I let Caleb have his cake and he dug right in. Needless to say, he had cake everywhere. It was the cutest thing I'd ever seen in my life. Watching my sweet little boy enjoy himself was surreal. Everyone had such a great time and I kept praising God thanking Him for allowing us and Caleb to see his 1st birthday. Happy 1st birthday Caleb!

2

BETRAYAL

It was time for Caleb's surgery and we needed to head up there a few days before he was scheduled for surgery. They needed to run tests and gather all the information before his operation. The doctors had never seen Caleb and they wanted to meet him before. I had called ahead of time and the Ronald McDonald's told me that they had a room for us. That was such a relief. They explained because of the distinct they always try to make accommodations for the families. The next two days were full of doctor's appointments and tests. John and I had lots of anxiety being so far away from home. We had no idea what to expect for this next open-heart surgery.

It was time for the appointment to meet Dr. H. He was so nice and very smart. During the appointment he went over what his plan was once he got into Caleb's chest. He had everything mapped out. He was going to discontinue the pulmonary arteries and connect a shunt from innominate artery so that he could re-establish blood flow to Caleb's left lung and it would be able to grow. He said this is going to be a very lengthy surgery because Caleb had clots in his artery and in that lung. He explained he would have to go in and clean everything out. He explained that he would be cleaning out all the clots in his lungs. After talking with the doctor even though I was scared he made things feel a little better because of his extensive plan. I knew God had placed Caleb in the best hands to get things fixed.

The day was here, and it was time to take Caleb for surgery. Of course, Caleb was the first case. The anxiety and fear was very overwhelming. But we were trying to be strong for Caleb. We tried to hide how we were feeling because Caleb was one and a half now. He was older and was starting to understand a little better. If he were to get upset and start crying, he would hold his breath and turn blue almost a purple. We told the doctors about this, so they decided that it would be in Caleb's best interest if we accompanied down to the surgery ward. They realized if Caleb went into one of his spells that could cause further damage to Caleb's organs and brain.

Here we go preparing to send our little boy into his third open heart surgery. The reality was a bit overwhelming. John and I realized that this surgery was very important, and that blood flow had to be established to his left lung. Without blood flow to both lungs it would be highly unlikely that Caleb would be a candidate for the last surgery (Fontan) or even a heart transplant. There was no way we could let that happen.

We headed to the surgery ward. Again, there we were those elevator doors. We entered in but this time it wasn't brightly lit. Actually, it was dim and kind of gloomy. My heart started racing. There was the throw up feeling again. I was so nervous I became clammy. I was trying to focus on Caleb, but everything was hazy. I was trying so hard to snap out of it because I knew if Caleb could tell I was upset he'd go into a crying spell and we did want that. Caleb looked at me and as hard as it was I put the biggest smile on my face and told him I loved him. The elevator opened and there were the doors that lead into the surgery room. You know the ones all the times before we had to stop at. Not this time we went straight passed them right into the room where Caleb would have surgery. Everyone was standing around and smiling as we entered in the room. The room was very bright. All the utensils and machines were all set up for Caleb. The anesthesiologist was there waiting by the bed we needed to lay Caleb on, so he could gas him off to sleep. We helped put Caleb onto the bed. Everything was moving so fast I could hardly get my bearings. As we laid Caleb on the bed we whispered prayer over him and the surgical team. We hugged and kissed Caleb. Caleb was scared with all that he was seeing. I tried to comfort him and tell him everything would be ok and to relax. He started to squirm and tried to get off the bed. John and I held him down as the doctor put the mask on his face. Caleb tried to put up a fight and hold his breath but, not for long. He took a deep breath and that's when his body went limp. The gas had taken over and Caleb was knocked out. I know you're thinking that is cruel. But John and I decided that if anyone was going to hold him down at a time like that it was going to be us and not strangers. If Caleb was to die at least the last touch and faces he saw would be ours. As crazy as that sounds it was very comforting for us.

What a crazy sight. I couldn't believe that we just did that. I was trying to get myself together as we were escorted to the waiting room by this fabulous person who introduced herself. Her name was Pam. She was amazing! She was funny and kept reassuring us that Caleb was in good hands. Pam told us that if there was anything we needed while we waited to please let her know. We settled in and waited. After a few hours we hadn't got an update, so Pam called back to see what was going on. They told her that they had all the lines in and that Caleb was open. They said the doctor had just got there and was just beginning the surgery. They also told us Caleb was doing great and he was stable. What was crazy before we wouldn't have known what that update meant but now that we had been at this for a while we knew exactly what all that meant. We settled back in and waited.

Hours passed, and the tension grew as we waited for some kind of update but there was nothing. I was praying so hard asking God to have mercy on Caleb and to guide the doctors to fix my broken little boy. Every time the phone would ring my heart would race was that the call? Was Caleb ok? Did something happen? And Finally, the call. They told us that there were even more clots then they had anticipated and cleaning them all out took a little longer than they thought. They told us Caleb was doing great and stable. Again, we settled in and more hours passed. It had to have been five maybe six hours by now! Then the phone rang and the call telling us that Caleb would be coming out of surgery and that the doctor would be out to talk to us shortly.

Pam showed us the room we needed to go and wait for Dr. H. The room was very tiny it had a few chairs in it and a box of tissue. A box of tissue I thought to myself. I bet there have been lots of tears cried in this room some for joy and so many of the news that their child didn't do well. We sat and waited for what seemed like an eternity and finally Dr. H came in to talk to us. His face looked very perplexed. He explained what he had done during the surgery. He told us he had everything connected, Caleb was doing great, and when he began to close Caleb he went into V-tach (ventricular tachycardia). Dr. H explained he had to shock him out of it. Then he said he went into V-tach again and had to once again be shocked out of it. Dr. H said he wasn't sure what had happened. He said during the entire surgery he never touched his heart. Dr. H said they were running test to figure out what was going on. He told us he didn't close

Caleb's chest up that he left him open just in case it happened again. He wanted to be able to get to Caleb's heart quickly. This was the worst news yet. I was crippled with fear. I was shaking and could barely stand up. I couldn't believe the next time I would see Caleb I would be able to see his heart beating in his chest. He told us Caleb was back in his room and that we would be able to see him soon. I couldn't believe what my ears were hearing. Caleb was in trouble again. This surgery was supposed to fix him not make him worse.

The time finally came, and we could see Caleb. I asked the nurse if they could cover his chest because I was unsure if I could handle seeing that, I thought staples were scary now I would be able to see his actual heart. I was terrified as we walked in the room where Caleb was. I walked up to the bed where he was laying. He didn't look so good. He was very puffy and had a gray tinge to him. I noticed the tree of medications going in him. I began to count them. 19 different medications running into my baby to keep Caleb alive. I can't lie I was devastated and couldn't believe that this was really happening. In my heart it really seemed like Caleb wasn't going to make it passed this one. I had to walk out of the room because I couldn't hold myself together. John followed me. We both embraced one another and just cried. No words there was nothing to say. We just tried to brace ourselves for what we thought was coming. God, how could this be happening?

Throughout the evening test results came rolling in. That's when we met Dr. W. She was the cardiologist working that night. She was looking over the results of Caleb's echo and saw that his heart wasn't perfusing properly. Dr. W was puzzled. The only logical explanation was during the surgery somehow his coronary artery was occluded. Dr. W stayed by Caleb's side the entire night tweaking meds and trying to piece together what happened during the surgery. The team finally came to the conclusion first thing in the morning they would be taking Caleb into the cath lab to see if they could open up his coronary artery. They thought that somehow a calcified clot was blocking the artery. John and I were standing there watching all of this unfold. It was the craziest thing we had ever seen. Stanford was different then Loma Linda we didn't have to leave while Caleb was intubated. We could stay by his side the whole entire time. I don't know if that was such a good thing. I think I was more traumatized watching all of this with my own eyes instead of having it explained to me. Either way it was hard to take in. Caleb was sick and truly fighting for his life now.

The morning came fast. We were up bright and early to meet with Dr. P. He had all the forms ready to be signed and get Caleb into the cath lab before any further damage was done to his heart. We walked with Caleb as they wheeled him to the cath lab. We prayed over Caleb and the surgical staff and away Caleb went. My heart was broken. Caleb was in grave danger and I was praying Dr. P would be able to fix my sweet little boy.

We waited in the waiting room. Our minds were racing. John suggested we take a walk down to the cafeteria. We gave Pam our numbers and said call us right away if you hear anything. John grabbed something to eat and I got something to drink. We hurried we didn't want to be gone long just in case anything happened. Not that we could fix anything but just being there made us feel a little better. Right as we were done heading back we just happened to run into Dr. H. That was crazy! He said he was glad he found us. He told us that they were unable to get through the coronary artery and that Caleb would have to go back into surgery. Dang, that wasn't what we wanted to hear. We replied ok when? Dr. H said he's on his way right now as he handed us the consent forms and asked if we could sign them. Our hearts sunk, I started to cry. To think that our son was on his way back to another open-heart surgery. This made four now and two in less than twenty-four hours. Now all the different thoughts came flooding through my mind were we really going to lose Caleb this time. I realized that Caleb was in grave danger and surgery was the only way to fix him. We signed the consent forms and away Dr. H went to save Caleb's life. John and I stood there watching Dr. H scurry away. Devastated isn't the word. I can't even tell you what either one of us felt. John just hugged me, and we slowly headed back to the waiting room.

I sat there praying but in the back of my head I was so afraid that I wasn't ever going to see or be able to hold my precious little boy ever again. Waiting was what we had come accustom to because Caleb was so complicated. Hours passed we received a few updates that Caleb was stable and doing well. We tried pretending we were ok but I'm sure all the staff knew we weren't. They were all so kind and kept checking on us. Finally, the call came that Dr. H would be out soon to meet with us. We went into the tiny room again. I grabbed tissue because I knew this time for sure I was going to need it.

Finally, the very tired looking Dr. H came in to talk to us. He had no expression on his face. It was so hard to get a read of the next words out of his mouth were going to be good or bad. He explained that there was a stitch right by his coronary artery. He wasn't sure when it was placed. Dr. H said that once he had completed the surgery and connected the shunt it caused his heart to shift and Caleb's artery to kink around the stitch. That stitch was what was stopping his heart for getting the oxygenated blood it needed. Dr. H explained he took down all the things he had done previously because Caleb's heart had suffered some damage. Leaving the shunt connected would only cause his heart to work harder and at this time we needed his heart to relax and recover from the very big hit it took when that happened. Dr. H said that he patched the coronary artery and that it looked beautiful. Now it was a waiting game to see how Caleb would do over the next few days. My heart sunk once again. The realization that my son had a heart attack which caused damaged. Caleb only has half a heart how much can his little heart endure? I broke down and called out to God asking him to have mercy on Caleb. I was trying very, very hard to comprehend all those things the doctor had just told us. Dr. H said Caleb was a very strong little boy to have survived this. He said the nurse would be out very soon and we could go in and see Caleb.

The nurse came, and we were able to go see Caleb. Walking into the room we encounter the same thing, so many different medications going into him. All the different monitors hooked up watching every little thing very closely. It was so hard as a mother to watch your baby going through all of this and I felt so helpless. Mothers are supposed to be able to kiss it and make it all better and I couldn't. Caleb's life was in God's hands and I just had to trust God. Even as much as I wanted Caleb to live I knew we needed a miracle and that was all up to God. Knowing the next forty-eight hours were very crucial and all we could do was wait and pray.

Caleb got through the night but still wasn't out of the woods. The next day we just sat beside Caleb hoping and praying. The nurse put us on bubble watch. With all the medications Caleb was on it was impossible to get all the air out of the IV lines so we would sit there and tap them out. Really what else were we going to do? So, we sat and watched. Sitting there my curiosity got the better of me and I finally got up the courage and wanted to look under the blanket that was covering Caleb's chest. The nurse described what it was going to look like and slowly moved the cover away. I know my eyes had to have been big. There it was a valley full of blood covered with something that looked like a big clear sticker. It was probably two inches wide. I could see straight into Caleb's body. There it was Caleb's heart beating. It was the craziest thing I had ever seen. I could actually see my son's heart beating right in front of my own eyes. Wow! That is all I could think was Wow!

The doctors were getting very concerned because Caleb wasn't peeing like they wanted him to. Because Caleb's heart had taken such a big hit they were worried kidneys might have been affected and weren't functioning properly. Doctor's had to change some medications around and add a stronger diuretic in hopes Caleb would start peeing on his own. Oh, my! His kidneys not functioning properly? I started praying asking God to please help Caleb's kidney function. Shortly after that, Praise God Caleb finally started to pee like they wanted him to. We all were so excited we all started doing the pee pee dance. I know its seems a little crazy but when you have a very sick little baby you realize how important peeing and pooping is. That was a miracle happening right before our very eyes. God had answered my prayers and Caleb's kidneys were working!

Another day passed, and Caleb seemed to be improving until the nurse noticed Caleb's feet was kind of cold to the touch and his oxygen levels weren't quite where they should be. She told the doctors of her concerns. The doctor's ordered an x-ray stat. The x-ray revealed that Caleb's left lung had collapsed. Yes, I said collapsed. Like we hadn't been through enough now Caleb's lung had collapsed. They weren't sure why, so they 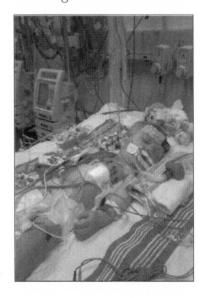 ordered an ultrasound stat. We needed to figure out why Caleb's lung was down and get it back up quickly before we had anything else happen. The ultrasound showed them that Caleb's left diaphragm was not working properly and that was what was causing his left lung to collapse. Shocked, yes this was a nightmare. Not only did my baby just have two open-heart surgeries in less than twenty-four hours now his diaphragm wasn't working causing his lung to collapse. This had to be a nightmare and we were going to wake up at any moment.

How was this happening we didn't understand so the doctor's explained that during open-heart surgeries there is a nervous system around the heart area and sometimes during surgery it can cause problems like this. We asked so how do we fix this? The doctor's explained Caleb would require another surgery called a plication which in layman's terms they will have to make an incision under the rib on Caleb's lower back and tuck the diaphragm down. This will correct the problem and keep the lung from continuing to collapse. We already had two open-heart surgeries since we have been here and now another one? You have to be kidding me? But they weren't! We had no choice if we wanted Caleb to live.

The doctor's explained that Caleb was recovering well and that although the surgery was a risk they believed Caleb would do just fine. The nurse got everything ready and Caleb headed to surgery. We walked with him down to the surgery area. We prayed for him and the staff. We stood there is disbelief and watched them take Caleb back. I was so numb. Whatever could have gone wrong with this visit had. I felt like I was at my breaking point. How much more could Caleb take? Was I being selfish now at this point praying for God to save my baby? Should I be praying that God would have mercy on my son and just take him back to Heaven? I had no Idea what I should pray for at that moment, so I just said never the less Your will Lord not mine!

We made our way back to the waiting room. My nerves were shot, and I kept having anxiety attacks. I was still trying to wrap my head around the fact that my little boy was on his way back to yet another surgery. We sat in the waiting room trying to stay optimistic about what the doctor's said. They said that Caleb would be ok. As a parent though you still can't help but to be scared because the reality was that Caleb might not be. We had set in for what we thought would be a long wait but to our surprise the entire surgery didn't even take two hours. The call came in that the doctor would be in soon to talk to us. That was crazy but great. Caleb's surgeries never go that quick! That news lifted our spirits a little.

The doctor came and explained that the surgery was a success and that Caleb held up like a "champ". The Doctor explained as soon as he tucked the diaphragm down Caleb's lung opened right back up. That was the best news we had heard in days! He also told us that it was working a little still and that with time it would start working again on its own. Another piece of great news. I was rejoicing. I started to cry, but this time I was crying happy tears.

Days passed, and Caleb was getting a little better every day. The nurse noticed Caleb had a cloudy like substance coming out of his chest tubes. It is called chylothorax which can develop after a traumatic event the lymph nodes dump a fatty substance into the pleural space in your body and the only way to fix it is to reduce the amount of fat intake. Like Caleb wasn't sick enough now we had to limit his fat intake. Now Caleb was only allowed five grams of fat a day. Ugh, I thought he is already so tiny he didn't even weigh 20lbs. Awesome how was Caleb going to regain his strength and get better on only five grams a fat a day?

Caleb's chest was still open, but Caleb's swelling was going down and there had been talk of closing his chest. That was great Caleb seemed to be moving in the right direction if they were considering closing his chest. I asked if they would be taking him back to the surgery area? They replied no we are just going to make his room sterile and close it up right in here. I was shocked, but they are the doctor's! So that is just what they did. It took about an hour. Once Dr. H was finished he came to talk to us. He explained that they were able to close him up nicely and Caleb did great. He also told us they had just performed an echo and that Caleb's heart showed some improvement in the function and that was a very good sign that Caleb would recover from this. Dr. H said Caleb was a very strong boy and that over the next few days he would be trying to get him off the vent. John and I were so grateful to hear that news we went out for a nice dinner to celebrate!

As the days progressed Dr. H was right, Caleb did get better. They were able to get him off the breathing tube. That's when we knew we had turned the corner and he was headed in the right direction. The only thing was that Caleb still could only have five grams of fat, so he was losing weight. It was taking a little longer than usual to get the chylis all cleared up.

Caleb progressed very quickly. To our surprise he was doing so well he was ready to be transferred out of the CVICU into the step-down unit. I was praising God that He had once again saved our son. After being transferred Caleb was doing great until I was getting ready to feed him, he started shaking and went into this crazy like seizure activity. I was talking to Caleb and all of a sudden, his eyes rolled into his head and his whole body got stiff. I was so scared I panicked and ran out of the room telling the nurses as I ran past them what was happening. I ran so fast heading down to the CVICU to get Dr. H. I thought Caleb was dying, I thought he was having another heart attack. As I entered the CVICU I found Dr. H I told him what was happening with Caleb and we ran to Caleb's room, so he could see. All I could think was we had already come so far and for him to leave now?

Dr. H looked over Caleb. He said Caleb isn't having a heart attack. He asked the nurses when was the last time Caleb had any pain medication. They said he hasn't! They explained that when children come up here we don't usually give them any. Dr. H was very unhappy. He explained Caleb had been through so many major surgeries that he had to be weaned off the narcotics. Caleb had become dependent on them and needed to be slowly tapered off. He told the nurse to get him a dose of Ativan right away. As soon as she gave Caleb the dose his body relaxed, and he was able to relax. Dr. H looked at his chart and made sure all his medications were ordered correctly. As he left he instructed the staff to make sure all of Caleb's medication be administered on time so that this wouldn't happen again. Unfortunately, because Caleb had that narcotic seizure his eyes went crossed. I learned at that time when a traumatic incident happens that can happen to anyone. My poor baby. After all he had been through now his eyes were crossed. I couldn't believe it, but I was so thankful he was still here. We just figured now we will add an eye doctor to Caleb's list and deal with that later.

Days passed, Caleb got better and better! The doctors told us that it was time and that we were finally able to make our journey back home. Home? We were able to take Caleb home? I called Ashley right away to tell her the good news! We would be on our way home soon. Wow! After all that Caleb had been through so close to death many times during that visit we were finally able to take Caleb home! Now that was a true Miracle!

At home Caleb was still on a low-fat diet. Caleb had the NG tube back in his nose. After all he had been through he had forgotten how to eat. His hair was falling out because he wasn't receiving enough fat in his diet it was so sad. Caleb was still detoxing from the narcotics. The doctors had him on a very slow taper because they didn't want that to happen again. That is one of the hardest thing's after a surgery is watching your child detox. I was like a walking zombie again. So many sleepless nights Caleb had medication he had to receive every three hours. I added thick-it to his milk again working on trying to get him to eat on his own. I am happy to say with a lot of work Caleb was off all the narcotics, and slowly but surely everything returned to normal again. Thank God. There was one thing that I noticed Caleb was choking much more now when he swallowed. I contacted the ENT doctor. She ordered another swallow study stat. Within a few days Caleb did the study. The study revealed Caleb's left vocal cord was partially paralyzed. She said that probably happened during the last stay in the hospital. The doctor told us he would have to have a surgery and that's when it would be corrected. Once the surgery was done Caleb would stop choking.

I made an appointment with the eye doctor right away to see what we could do to correct Caleb's eye. We went to the appointment and the doctor suggested we try a patch. I tried using a patch to see if that would strengthen his eyes but unfortunately it didn't. I called the doctor after several weeks and reported it didn't help. She told us there was a surgery that would correct it. She explained the surgery doesn't take long but he would have to go under anesthesia. After all that Caleb had been through we knew any time Caleb goes under there is a risk. The eye doctor said we needed a cardiac clearance form his cardiologist. We made appointments and talked to Dr. B on the risks and benefits. Dr. B said after the last echo he did Caleb's heart was getting stronger. He thought the surgery would be ok and would help him as well developmentally. We got the answer's we were looking for. Dr. B gave us the thumbs up, so I scheduled to have the surgery done.

Just as things seemed to be falling into place and we were managing to have some kind normalcy we received a call from Dr. H. He explained to us what exactly happened during Caleb's surgery. When the fellow was opening Caleb to prepare him for surgery he accidentally cut Caleb's coronary and placed the stitch. So, when Dr. H connected the shunt Caleb's coronary kinked around that stitch. Dr. H told us that after reviewing the echo Caleb's left pulmonary artery was occluded and the only pulmonary flow Caleb was getting to his left lung was from collateral veins his body had made to keep his lung alive. Dr. H explained that it was very crucial we bring Caleb back for another open-heart surgery to reestablish flow to his left lung. He told us that if we didn't it would cut the life expectancy very short and he probably would not be a candidate for the Fontan or a transplant for that matter. Dr. H told us as hard as it is that we had to put our feelings aside and do what was best for Caleb. That was not the phone call we ever expected to get. We had to make a choice. John and I agreed but asked Dr. H if he would be the only one to open and close Caleb a term known as skin to skin we would agree. He promised that he would. So, we said ok. Dr. H told us he would get Caleb on the schedule as soon as possible. We hung up the phone in shock. Open heart number five? Was this really happening?

So away we went back to Stanford. The trip was very difficult, but we made our way. The morning came, and we headed to the hospital for Caleb's fifth open heart surgery. We followed the staff. We prayed over Caleb and the surgery team. We held Caleb as they gassed him off to sleep. Again, as hard as it was we had to let Caleb go. After we walked out of the room I had a little meltdown and John did his best to try to comfort me, but our relationship was not as strong as it once had been. We were becoming more and more distant. We made our way to the waiting room and of course Pam was there. It was always great seeing her and she was always such a comfort. So, we were playing the waiting game again. As we waited we got several updates that Caleb was doing great and stable. After about five hours we got the call that Dr. H would be in very soon. After about thirty minutes he came in. Dr. H's face was always so emotionless it was hard to tell exactly what was going on. Was he going to tell us good news or was he going to tell us something we didn't want to know?

Dr. H explained that Caleb did great through the surgery. He explained looking at his heart function he thought that Caleb's heart would recover from what had happened the last surgery. That was such great news. Dr. H went on to explain how he had connected the shunt from the innominate artery in a downward slope so that hopefully it would help from clotting. He also explained he wanted to add blood thinners to "keep the wheels greased" so it would help keep everything open and flowing. Man, this was the greatest news yet. A little nervous about the blood thinners because Caleb was a very active little boy but if that's what we needed to do to keep Caleb's lung receiving blood, then so be it. Dr. H said because Caleb had done so well he was going to let him rest for the evening and in the morning, he was going to get him off the vent. Wow, that was shocking but so great. The next day just like Dr. H said Caleb was off the vent and doing great. Every day that passed Caleb got better and better and within eight days we were discharged from the hospital and we were on our way home.

Once we were home we tried to get as back to normal as we could. Ashley was getting ready to graduate from high school. I was trying to juggle all of these things. I wasn't doing such a great job because Caleb took up so much of my time. Caleb was becoming an obsession to me. Constantly checking everything; is he eating, is his color good, is he peeing and pooping, and making sure all his meds were on time was all my days consisted of.

All my other relationships were suffering because of it. I was trying my best but not doing such a great job. As the time went on John and I weren't getting along, and our relationship was getting worse and worse. I was miserable, and I knew he was as well. I suggested counseling, but he wasn't wanting to do that. I thought he was working too much and maybe needed to go do something good. We had already bought tickets to a baseball game that John wanted to go to, but I remembered John mentioning that it was one of his best friend's birthdays that week, so I suggested that instead of me going it could be a guy's night! I figured that might be good for him since we didn't have much normalcy since Caleb had been born. So of course,

John agreed and called three of his other guy friends and set it all up. As the game got closer one of his friends realized he wouldn't be able to go and so his girlfriend was going to take his ticket instead. Then one of his other friend wasn't able to attend so his friend's girlfriend brought one of her cousins. I thought that's fine because it was her guy cousin.

Game time finally got here, and John got ready to go and picked up the two other friends on his way down to the game and the friend whose birthday it was, was going to meet them there. So, me being me I called to make sure John was ok. He was acting funny when we were talking so I asked so who ended up going with you? He reassured me it was his buddies girlfriend and her "guy cousin". I said are you sure because you are sure acting funny. He reassured me that it was and said I was overre-acting. The day went by and I was hoping he was having a great time with his friends. The night came, and it was getting later and later and still John wasn't home.

Around 2am I called him to find out where he was. He said he was dropping them off and that they ran into a lot of traf-fic. He told me he would be home soon. What was weird was he said he was in the car, but I heard the bell that rings when you first get in after you put in your keys. I tried to dismiss it, but my gut was telling me something was up. John finally got home around 4am. I said that was sure a lot of traffic. He said we needed to talk but I replied there wasn't much to say. I was hurt and didn't want to talk.

The morning came early, and Caleb was up and ready to eat. Once I fed Caleb he went back to sleep. I went outside to get something in the truck and that's when I found it. I found a camera inside a sock. I thought one of his friends must have left it. So of course, because he had gotten home so late I thought I'm just going to look at the pictures to see what's in there. Once I turned the camera on there they were. The pictures of his buddy's girlfriend and another girl. My heart sunk, and I felt as if I was going to throw up. Then it all hit me that's why he was acting funny all day. And then it really hit me why all the lies? Why did he lie about who was with him? What was really going on?

I waited for him to wake up because I knew if I stormed in there it would have made things worse. I went into our room and asked him. So, are you going to tell me the truth now? Of course, he acted dumb and answered "about"? I said who went to the game with you? John replied I was never going to tell you the truth. He said because he knew I would act like this. But who wouldn't especially after all the lies? I was crying so hard I couldn't believe it! John asked how did you find out? I replied your "guy cousin" left her camera in the car. I said I should throw it in the trash! John got super defensive and said give me the camera I'll make sure it gets back to her. I was so heartbroken. I asked him what happened were you with her. Of course, he said no but, in my heart, I knew.

I tried to get over it. Ashley and John were finally getting along so good and I knew I really depended on John for so much. But I couldn't do it. Even though he said he didn't do anything I knew in my heart he had been unfaithful to me. I was trying to believe him, but everything just got worse I could feel myself sinking into a depression. It was bugging me, so I asked him again what had happened? John said I'm not going to reassure you anymore because you're going to believe what you want. That was the final straw for me. I had enough. I told John I have put up with so much over the years and I take such great care of our son but that I can't deal with. After a huge argument, I put Caleb in the car and told him I'm leaving. You have three hours I want you out of here. I was crushed but there was no way I could live with a liar anymore and it was time for us to be apart. So, we left!

I went to my best friend Michelle's house, I was such a mess. She was trying to comfort me but there was no comforting me. It felt like my world was closing around me. I couldn't believe that this was happening how could he betray us like this. Not only did I have a special needs child, now my marriage was falling apart. All I kept thinking was how am I going to do this? I knew I couldn't work outside of the home because Caleb needed so much. How was I going to be able to handle this? How was I going to be a single mom again with a very sick little boy? How would I be able to take care of us?

The three hours had passed, Caleb and I made our way home. I walked in the door and sure enough John had packed all his stuff and left. Now the reality set in and I was crushed, all I could do was cry! It hurt so bad. I felt so lost without him there, I depended on him for so much.

Days passed, I tried reaching out to John, but it was very apparent that our relationship was over, and he was done. We now had to figure out how we were going to co-parent. We had to decide how he was going to help me support Caleb. Not a conversation I ever anticipated having but one that we needed to have. John called all the shots. He decided I would keep the truck and he would make the payments in lieu of giving me child support. I explained that the truck was too expensive and that there was no way I could afford a vehicle like that. I tried having him take it, but he said he didn't want it. He wasn't trying to see it from my point of view. He had made up his mind and that was it! I couldn't afford the truck and as much as I hated it I had to let the truck go.

I was trying to be wise so before they came to get the truck I purchased a new car that made sense for Caleb and I. A car was better for Caleb and me especially because of all the back and forth to doctor's appointments. I can't lie this was so hard I was so broken. I hurt so bad that I honestly didn't think I was going to make it through this. It even hurt to breath. I was in a depression and could barely eat. Every time I saw John it made it harder. They were a couple now and everyone knew it. I was so humiliated. I didn't understand why he chose her over me, but the reality was he did, and I had to except it.

Time passed, and I knew I needed help, so I got counseling trying to wrap my head around what was my life going to be now? With her help I started to except what happened. The truth was John had found someone and he wanted to be with her. I had a very hard time accepting that. I had all the questions: What did I do wrong? What was wrong with me? You know all the questions that cross your mind when you have a break up and it's for someone else. As much as I wished it didn't happen it did. I had no choice but to suck it up and keep moving on as best I could. One day at a time. I had to figure out who I was now without John not so easy to do when your consumed with a special needs child.

We tried getting visitations set up. John was a little nervous to have Caleb alone overnight because he had never taken care of him on his own I was always there. He started by taking Caleb for a few hours and gradually he took him more and more. We weren't seeing eye to eye on the visitation and support John had his own idea and I had mine. I was so tired of fighting about it, so it was just best to get the courts and child support involved. I thought we could figure it out, but the truth was I was so hurt and becoming bitter about the whole situation it was wise to let them figure it all out for us so that it would be fair across the board.

We had to go to mediation and try to resolve our issues. I can't lie I was hurt and wasn't the easiest to deal with, but neither was he. We went to court and got everything settled. John agreed to three weekends a month and the judge told us he would determine the child support according to the California State guidelines. So that part was settled and now back to life co-parenting Caleb. Things went a little smoother. We still struggled with things but at least there was a schedule and he was spending more time with Caleb.

It came time to get Caleb's eyes fixed. Our first surgery not being together as a couple. I wondered how that would be? We went to Caleb's pre-op appointment, so the eye doctor could go over what the plan was for the day of the surgery. John and I decided to drive together in the same car. Probably not the best idea. We were ok at first but of course we began to fuss a little at one another. We never really addressed anything and now we were. Ugh! The truth's he was revealing to me hurt so bad. To hear that John didn't love me anymore and that he was in love with someone else hurt me to my core. All I could do was cry. As I sat there listening to the words I never wanted to hear come out of his mouth! He told me he wanted a divorce. My heart shattered as those words came flying out. He told me he was in love with her and didn't want to be married to me anymore. Definitely not the day I had hoped for, but it was what he wanted so I had no choice but to give it to him.

We got to the appointment I had to put on my happy face like all that didn't just happen on the drive down there. We sat there, and the doctor went over what was going to happen during the procedure. The visit was over, and it was time to head home. I tried my best to keep my emotions in check, but it was hard. I didn't want him to see that he had broken me. John drove we didn't exchange much words. I was afraid he would tell me more about how happy he was and how much he loved her, so it was best to just keep my mouth shut. John dropped himself off, I took over and drove home. I was so crushed with all that I was told that day and cried all the way home.

The day came for Caleb to get his eyes fixed. After what had happened the last time we drove together I decided it would be best if we just met at the hospital. We both arrived at the same time and prepared for the surgery. Things were so different this time. Everything seemed so cold between John and me. I tried to focus on Caleb but inside I was hurting so bad. It was time for Caleb to go back and as always, we walked with Caleb went into the room. Everyone was so happy. We laid Caleb down as they placed the mask on and gassed him to sleep. John and I made our way to the waiting room. The tension was very thick. I wasn't sure what to do. John and I always talked and comforted one another during this time. Thankfully it wasn't an open-heart. We sat quiet and waited. The doctor came out after a short time and said the surgery went well and Caleb was in recovery. She told us we could see him soon.

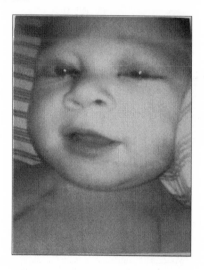

The nurse came out and we went to go see Caleb. My poor guy's eyes were all red and swollen. The doctor said once he was fully awake and was able to eat and drink we could go home. I was nervous and asked John if he wanted to come to my house and help me because I didn't know what the evening would bring, and I hadn't been alone caring for Caleb after surgery. John declined so Caleb and I made our journey home. John asked if I could keep him updated. I was a little angry because I thought he should be there, but it was his choice. I sent him updates and pictures, so he could see what was going on. Caleb had a great night and woke up in the morning to what seemed like a whole new world for him. He was looking around in amazement like it was his first time seeing the world. It was so exciting. I was so happy for Caleb. My baby could finally see the right way.

A few days passed, and it was time for our follow up appointment at eye doctor, so she could check out Caleb's eyes. The appointment went great and the doctor was pleased. The doctor did explain that in a few years she may have to repeat the surgery because as Caleb grew his eyes would change and might need to be corrected again.

As the time drew closer for his next open-heart surgery Dr. H was determined to put Caleb back together the right way. He needed to do a heart catherization to see what was going on with Caleb's heart and arteries. I immediately scheduled the surgery. I made sure to warn the doctors about Caleb's serve allergy to fentanyl before surgery. Once the procedure was over and Caleb was in recovery he got extremely upset because he was in a lot of pain which triggered Caleb to have an event called ridged chest where he stopped breathing and turned very blue. The nurses and doctors rushed into action, bagging Caleb to get him breathing again trying to raise his oxygen levels back up. His heart rate bottomed out and made his oxygen level drop all the way down to 33%. The doctors and nurses worked so hard to make Caleb stable. That was a very scary time as it was just me and my cousin Marianne because John was away at work out of state. I wasn't sure what would have caused my son to have an event like this. When the doctor and anesthesiologist came to check on him, that's when I had found out she had given him fentanyl. I asked her why she would do such a thing and she replied, "I didn't think that he was allergic." It made me so very angry! It took everything in me to keep my composure. The doctor was so angry but there was nothing we could do because the damage was already done. Needless to say, because of her mistake an outpatient procedure turned in to an overnight stay in the hospital.

Once we got Caleb upstairs in the CVICU everything was going great. Caleb was back to his normal happy laughing self he was even eating his favorite snack Cheetos and then all of a sudden, he went into another spell. Here came the nurses and doctors running frantically into the room to work on Caleb again. It was so scary, and it was terrifying watching them working on him it was like a bad episode on a medical TV show.

I was all alone then watching my son fight for his life. With tears in my eyes I called John to let him know what was going on with our son. What seemed like an eternity but was only 10 minutes they finally got Caleb stabilized. I looked up to the Heaven and thanked God that my son was okay for now. I was outraged that this was even happening to him, and had she not given him the medicine my baby boy wouldn't be going through this. After that we had a quiet night with no more incidents and the next day Caleb was okay to go home. Before we left they made an appointment to do an EEG because they wanted to make sure that event didn't do any damage to Caleb's brain.

The next week Caleb had an appointment with sedation to check his brain. They gave him some medication to relax him. Because Caleb had, had so much medication in the past it took much more than they anticipated to get him to go to sleep. Caleb needed to be very still for this procedure, so they could get an accurate read. Once the procedure was done we could leave. Caleb was so out of it we went to John's place just till I felt comfortable going home with Caleb. After about three hours we made our way home. Once we got home Caleb rested. We got the results from the EEG and there wasn't any further damage from the episode. Thank God that was such a relief.

Caleb had been through so much in the past year, but can you believe it he was getting ready to turn two. It was nothing but a miracle that we even made it here. Again, I held out no stops. Caleb loved Sponge Bob so much I thought that would be the perfect theme. I invited all our family and friends to come and celebrate with us. Caleb was every excited to see everyone. As the party was getting under way I received a call from John informing me that he would be unable to attend. I was so disappointed but there was nothing that could be done about that. I was determined to have a great time and celebrate Caleb's birthday. The children were all playing. Everyone was talking and eating. I made tons of food. The time came, now we were going to sing happy birthday to Caleb. Everyone gathered around then we began to sing. Caleb was smiling ear to ear. I was elated to see how happy he was. As the song ended Caleb blew the candle out by himself. Everyone cheered! What a blessing Caleb had miraculously made it to his second birthday. Happy second birthday Caleb!

3

MIRACLE

Caleb was still receiving services from the Inland Regional Center. Theresa came once a week to work with Caleb and he was doing great. Caleb was reaching his milestones and developing life was getting easier. But, now we had to prepare for another surgery. Not again Caleb had already been through enough and there was still more. We hadn't even made it to the last stage surgery the Fontan. I got the phone call that arrangements had been made to get Caleb's next surgery done.

In the midst of all this John and I still could not seem to get along. It wasn't the fact that he had moved on, it was the fact that I felt he wasn't spending much time with Caleb. There were a lot of days where I felt like I was facing these obstacles by myself. As a parent we always try to put on a brave face for our children, when the truth is I was losing myself. I began to remember all of the parents I met throughout the years and how I wasn't alone. I knew I had to be strong for Caleb no matter what because I was blessed to have him with me for these 2 years. He was my strength.

We headed up to Stanford. Caleb had to have test ran before

surgery. When the tests were done we went back to the room to get some rest as we knew the next day would be a big one. We got up early and made our way to the hospital. Once we got to the hospital Caleb realized where we were and though he had little words you could tell on his face exactly what he was feeling. All the doctors came by and went over all what they were doing. They always have to tell you the worst-case scenario. Then make you sign the paperwork to allow them to do what they needed to do. A few minutes before time to go they always give Caleb a little something to take the edge off so he won't be so scared. Once the medication started kicking in it was time to go. Once we were in the room we prayed over Caleb. Then laid him on the table. We assisted in holding him until he received the gas and drifted off to sleep. This was getting harder and harder every time. Still we had no choice if we wanted Caleb to have some kind of quality of life.

John and I went up to our regular place to wait. Our bright star was at the desk. Pam was always there. So now we wait and wait and wait. This surgery seemed to go on and on. We got a few updates while we were waiting just the normal everything is going well, and that Caleb was stable. After about six hours we got the call Dr. H would be out soon. Thirty minutes later he finally came. He said the surgery was a success, and that he had already taken Caleb off the vent. What? That hasn't ever happened. The pervious surgeries had always taken such a toll on Caleb that it took days even weeks to get him off. This was a true miracle in itself. Dr. H explained that he had went in and done all the things he needed to do with no issues. Dr. H said Caleb is so strong he's probably going to outlive us all. Wow! That was music to our ears. He left us with you will be able to go in and see him soon.

John and I looked at each other with amazement. I think we were in shock because that had never happened in the past. We were both ecstatic. I was praising God and John got on the phone to deliver the good news to everyone. We knew Caleb still had to get through the next 48 hours with no hiccups, but we were ready for what the next few days would hand us.

We were told we could go see our precious Caleb. As we headed in the room I was asking God to give us the strength to help Caleb and to guide us through these next few days. Caleb was very groggy but still managed to put a smile on his face when he saw John and I, tears streamed down our faces. What a beautiful sight. We were careful not to stimulate Caleb as he had just been through his 6th open heart surgery. Caleb was weak and needed to rest. We just sat by his bed quietly but inside I was overjoyed by what the day had brought. This was not something we were accustomed to. We geared up for what we knew was going to be a long night.

Caleb's nurse was amazing she stayed on top of everything and managed Caleb's pain wonderfully. Caleb was in great spirits. The doctor's rounded and were pleasantly surprised at what they saw. This was not our "normal" Caleb. He always keeps us on our toes as they laughed. Since Caleb is doing so well they all agreed unanimously that Caleb could have some water and if he could tolerate it we could progress slowly to food. I could hardly believe my ears. This was the craziest but most delightful news yet.

We started by giving Caleb a few sips to see how his tummy would handle it. We were very careful we didn't want Caleb to throw-up that would be horrible it had been less than 24 hours since the surgery. To our surprise Caleb did great. He was asking for more as he simultaneously knocked both his fists together as he used the sign language he had been taught. That was remarkable. I looked at the nurse as we made eye contact she said go ahead and give him more. I gave Caleb more and to our amazement he did great. As the day progressed doctors kept stopping by I think they were all buzzing about how well Caleb had done they truly wanted to see it with their own eyes.

By the evening Caleb was able to eat Jello and broth. We were heading in the right direction. Caleb was still weak but gaining his strength. He was getting back to the Caleb we were accustomed to. He kept asking to watch Yo Gabba Gabba and Sponge Bob. Caleb's chest tubes (these are placed to help keep the fluid from accumulating in the body) were not putting out much fluid so the doctor's said in the morning they would be removing them. They went on to say once they are removed they wanted Caleb up and out of the bed. Wow! Things were moving very quickly on this visit. I wasn't complaining this was just not "our norm". My soul was so overjoyed! I couldn't believe how smoothly this visit was going.

Caleb had a restful night and just as the doctor's said they removed the chest tube. After they were done with that they told us to order Caleb a hearty breakfast as he would be needing it they wanted him up and walking after he was done. Whew! Ok! I got on the phone and ordered all of Caleb's favorite's. The breakfast arrived, and Caleb dug in. I was in a little shock that he just jumped right in, we let Caleb's tummy settle for a bit. Then we prepared him for his first walk. This was a bit tricky. Caleb still was hooked up to all the wires that monitored his heart plus all the IV's as we had not got the orders to transition to oral medications yet. We got everything ready and away we went. Caleb was doing great and waving at everyone who walked by and saying hi. He even gave a few knuckles. We just took a short walk I didn't want to push him too much.

As the days passed Caleb was back to his charming self. We had only been there a few days and there was already talk of sending Caleb home. Home? This was crazy! But, sure enough the doctor's rounded and said Caleb is doing so great we think we're going to send you home tomorrow. This really was the best news yet. We had only been in the hospital one week. John and I were delighted at this news and prepared to make our journey home.

The next morning all the discharge paperwork was ready. We packed Caleb up and headed to out. We made our stops thanking all the staff for everything they had done for Caleb during his stay. We all were in shock that Caleb was actually able to go home in eight days. As we departed all the doctors jokingly said we don't want to see you for a long time Caleb! But all the while hated to see him go everyone loved him so much! This was just another miracle to add to Caleb incredible journey.

We made it home safe and sound. We got back to our normal which consisted of visits from Theresa as we tried to get Caleb stronger and help him continue to reach his mile stones. Also, doctor visits to keep an eye on Caleb's heart and progression. I am happy to say other than the one open heart surgery Caleb was having a great year. We were actually able to relax and let Caleb enjoy life outside of those hospital walls.

October was fastly approaching and we needed to get ready for Caleb's third birthday. Can you believe it his third birthday? My heart was so thrilled to be planning it. What was the theme going to be? I was at the dollar store and that's when it hit me. I was going to do a Luau theme. I could just picture it all the boys in cool board shorts and all the little girls running around in grass skirts. I started getting all the decorations together. It was going to be over the top.

The day of the party. We were up early and started to transform the backyard into all I had envisioned. Guests started to arrive. I had food on the grill it smelled so amazing. Ashley, Erica, and Marianne put all the food out that we had prepared the night before. Everyone was having such a great time. The only thing that was missing was the cake. Michelle was running late, and she was the one who insisted on making Caleb his special cake. Finally, she arrived it was perfect! She did an amazing job! As she sat it down everyone gathered around. I lit the candles and began to sing happy birthday to Caleb. Caleb was so happy and smiling ear to ear. He blew the candles out and everyone cheered. We served the cake as the kids continued running around having a blast. What a great day! Happy third birthday, son!

4

EXHALE

After Caleb's third birthday I couldn't believe how well he was doing. He was showing us just how much of a fighter he was. It was really such a feeling of relief we could finally exhale for minute. Our lives seemed to be looking up Ashley was working a great job. My sessions with the therapist were really paying off. We were all just trying to figure out our purpose in life, I began focusing on my Non-profit and really getting things in order.

Everything was pretty amazing until one day Ashley came home from work feeling terrible. She had a really high fever, a nagging cough that sits in the chest and keeps you hacking away at night and disrupting your sleep. I didn't really think much of it I just wrote it off as the common cold. As much as I tried to prevent Caleb and I from contracting it, it was a failed effort.

He was miserable, his little body just couldn't take it. He had the chills, night sweats, nausea, and diarrhea. All I could do was make sure he was staying hydrated and make him as comfortable as possible. He must have taken at least four baths a day just trying to sooth all his aches and pains away. I didn't want whatever this bug was to cause Caleb any other worse illness that could cause him to be hospitalized, so I took him the urgent care, it turns out Caleb had the swine flu. I was so relieved that I took him when I did because his immune system was so weak it could have killed him. The doctors informed me that he was doing well and everything I did really helped his body fight the virus and, that they would prescribe him Tamiflu to help speed up the recovery process. Thankfully the flu didn't last long he was down for two weeks then right back to his joyful self.

The next month's flew by rather quickly Caleb was thriving and learning, I was so proud of him. I don't want to say things were perfect, but it was perfect for us. By now John and I were in a much better place he was visiting Caleb a lot more and we were arguing less. I began remembering who I was and started having more of a social life. I became an active member in church and got back in touch with God. I can honestly say things haven't been this normal in such a long time.

My organization Babies So Special was still underway so I wanted to have an event to keep the momentum going. Caleb was obsessed with the show Yo Gabba Gabba he loved the singing and dancing it was his favorite thing to do. That gave me the perfect idea to host a dance-A-thon, so many people came out it was such a beautiful and heartwarming feeling. People were dancing for their siblings and babies there was so much love in the air. We had three spectacular prizes, a four pack of Disney Land tickets, a pair of Los Angeles Angels Tickets and 100-dollar visa gift card. It felt like the whole community came out to support. I knew from that day this thing was going to be bigger than I ever imagined.

What a blessing it was time to get things together to celebrate Caleb's fourth birthday. Can you believe it! After all that life has thrown our way we had the honor to celebrate this special day. Since Caleb was so in love with Yo Gabba Gabba I knew the theme had to be that. I ordered him a DJ Lance Rock costume this year had to be perfect. I was so excited I could hardly wait to put it on him, I knew he was going to look so adorable. DJ Lance wore glasses, so I knew that was going to be a struggle to keep those on him but, we will cross that road when we get there. I got everything ready and sent out the invitations.

Before I knew it, it was the day of Caleb's fourth birthday. I was up early preparing the house for everyone's arrival. It was so fun decorating Caleb was my big helper. It was finally time to get Caleb dressed in his costume. He looked so cute! I was right though, Caleb wouldn't keep the glasses on his face. They were such an important piece I didn't know what to do then it dawned on me I got a black eye liner and drew them on his face. Now he looked perfect!

Everyone started to arrive, Caleb was so excited to see new faces. The kids played, and the parents stood around talking and enjoying the food I had prepared. It was time to sing happy birthday. We all gathered around the birthday boy as he blew out the candles. What a great end to an awesome year. Happy Fourth Birthday son!

5

FAMILY

Things were still going well with Caleb and it felt good seeing him enjoy life. Ashley had started a new job out on Fort Irwin and was considering moving to Irvine to attend school. I had even met a man from church and we really hit it off, his name was Derane. I was sort of hesitant about stepping back into the dating scene, I wasn't sure if I was ready. I mean let's be honest dating is hard enough, but when you bring kids in the mix it's downright complicated.

When he was around it was instant, you know the feeling you get when you just know someone is going to play a significant role in your life. That's what I felt with Derane I wasn't sure what that role was but whatever it was, it was important. I found myself walking around like a schoolgirl getting butterflies, did I really have a crush?

I didn't start dating Derane right away it took a battle within myself to accept that it was okay to step out and take chances. I was worried about being judged and everyone else's opinion of me. What would my kids think? Would they even like this guy. What about Caleb he was my main focus and I could not lose focus. I didn't want to feel like I was placing my time anywhere besides with Caleb. Not only was I afraid I would be abandoning Caleb, but I was still not over John. That part of me was still broken and no matter how many times I changed my hair or tried to start over I couldn't. There was still a lot of resentment and anger inside of me and even though I was seeking help through counseling and church there was no shaking it. I was still trying to wrap my head around that he didn't think I was good enough. No matter what efforts I put forth he chose her not me.

Derane already had four kids of his own so he was really understanding of how I felt. I had to really open myself up and remember, regardless of how my last relationship ended I couldn't fault him. I appreciated him for allowing me to be myself and treating me like a human being. Things escalated pretty quickly between him and I, there was just no escaping it. He made me feel something that I didn't even realize I was missing, it was really something special. It wasn't just me who really felt a connection with Derane, Caleb did too and that felt amazing. I really think he liked having that male figure around. We all began really hanging out as a blended family, Derane had some really cool kids.

The next few months were an exciting time for me. I found myself smiling more and regaining focus. Everything really seemed to be falling into place for us. Ashley was happy and thriving at work and school, Caleb's health was steady and looking hopeful. It was hard to imagine that just a few years ago I was ready to just give up. I was feeling so good my therapist said I graduated and no longer needed treatment. I had even introduced Derane to John and what I thought was going to be a disastrous situation turned out to be ok. Sure, we had a few bumps in the road but that's to be expected with blended families, you just learn to make it work.

Summer was here, and it was hot! Derane and I decided to take all of the kids to the water park. Ashley was even able to get the day off to join us. I was so nervous I know Caleb has been doing well but this was big. When we arrived, it was a lot for Caleb to take in all of the hustle and bustle and kids everywhere, I think I made him overwhelmed. Despite his feeling of uneasiness, he had a great time. I'm pretty sure he rode everything he possibly could, it was such a magical moment seeing he and Ashley really getting a chance to just be free. When we got home I made sure I bathed Caleb thoroughly because I knew he was literally swimming in germs. As I got Caleb all snuggled in and ready I looked back at how far my little guy has come. There were days when I never thought he would be able to even step foot into a water park. I was just eternally grateful at how far God has brought him.

We really felt like a complete family again, a real-life Brady Bunch. Derane and I were inseparable the kids were getting along and really adjusting to this new life. He would come over with the kids and we would have these huge sleepovers and play games. It was in moments like these that I knew it was only up from here.

Caleb was turning five soon and he was infatuated with pirates, so I decided to do a Jake and the neverland pirates theme. I was searching all over Pinterest for ideas I was really ecstatic to decorate for this party. I decided to turn the garage into pirate's cove. I knew Caleb and all the children were going to love it. I was on the computer ordering the decorations which included a Jake costume for Caleb. The day couldn't get her fast enough.

It was finally here Caleb's big day. It was time to make my vision a reality. I transformed my backyard table into a pirate ship, filled up a wading pool with sand and all sorts of hidden "treasure" for the kids to find. I also ordered a fog machine to give it that ghostly effect, we played stormy ocean music to have the perfect atmosphere.

Getting Caleb dressed was always the fun part I even gelled his hair, so he could look just drake. He was ready just in time as the first guest was due to arrive. He was so happy to see everyone, though he was a little standoffish of the kids at first. The other kids all ran and played but Caleb stayed back with me for a while. I had even prepared pirate themed food and there was a shark head made out of watermelon rinds and fruit in his mouth. After a few minutes or so Caleb finally relaxed and was able to enjoy his party.

His favorite part was here it was time to gather around and sing happy birthday. We all sang, and Caleb clapped his hands with utter excitement. Caleb blew out the candles as everyone cheered what a great day full of fun and pirate adventures. Happy Fifth birthday son!

6

DEVASTATION

Caleb was doing so well but it now came time for Dr. H to put Caleb back together the way he had planned originally. He needed the pulmonary arteries to be continuous and close any shunts. It was a frightening time as the past two years were so peaceful and we had a new family dynamic now. We knew we had no choice and that Caleb was still in God's hand and we had to trust Him no matter the outcome.

It was time to head back to Stanford but before we could go back Dr. H wanted us to get a cardiac angiogram to see how Caleb's vessels were doing and if his left pulmonary artery was open or if it had clotted again. Derane and I made our way to UCLA for this test because Loma Linda's equipment was not working. At UCLA John and I were with Caleb waiting to be taken back for the procedure. Caleb had to be sedated because he didn't understand how to lay still and for the images they needed Caleb wouldn't be able to move. They didn't allow us to go with Caleb this time. We prayed over Caleb and they took him back for the procedure. The procedure went very quickly. I stayed the night in UCLA because of the sedation, just to make sure Caleb was close to a hospital just in case he had an episode.

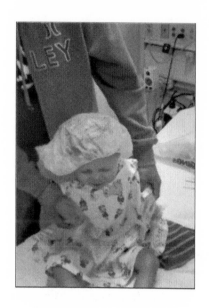

Caleb had a good night and we headed home. Once we were back home everything returned to normal. A few days later we got a call from Dr. H he wanted to go over the results of the test. I asked the doctor to hang on and I called John three way. Once John was on the line Dr. H told us that unfortunately Caleb had clotted off the left side of his pulmonary artery again. What a discouraging blow. Not again UGH! Caleb had already been through so much and to think its clotted again. This made it almost impossible to have the final stage surgery.

We both asked the doctor what now? Dr. H said he would try again but this time he would do a unifocalization. He explained that he would go through Caleb's back and get his vessels from the left lung and connect them all together. Then he would connect them to an artery and that would help them to grow. Once they grew and matured he would be able to reconnect the pulmonary and this would give Caleb a chance. A chance for the final surgery and make his chances for heart transplant greater. Another open-heart surgery. My poor little guy. But what other choice did we have? If we wanted Caleb to live and have a good quality of life, we had to do it. Dr. H said he would make the arrangements for the surgery.

We went up to our regular place to wait. Our bright star was at the desk. She was always there. So now we wait and wait and wait. This surgery seemed to go on and on. We got a few updates while we were waiting. Just the normal everything is going well, and that Caleb was stable. After about six hours we got the call Dr. H would be out soon. Thirty minutes later he finally came. He said the surgery was a success, but that Caleb had a long road ahead of him. His recovery wouldn't be easy, but it was up to Caleb now. We knew the next forty-eight hours would be very critical.

Caleb was back in his room we were able to see him. The doctors and nurses were settling Caleb in. I looked up and saw his numbers were bouncing all over the place. Caleb was coding. The nurse hit the code button, and everyone started rushing into Caleb's room. I jumped out of the way. I was terrified. I didn't know what to do so I ran out and called Camille so that we could pray. My body was filled with fear that my son might be leaving this world. After we prayed I went back into Caleb's room. The maddens had settled down. The doctor's discovered that during the transport back to the room Caleb's breathing tube had shifted and that only Caleb's right lung was receiving oxygen. They corrected it but not before Caleb's heart took another hit.

They ordered an echocardiogram right away. Caleb's lower left part of his heart wasn't functioning like it once had. The doctor's explained that they had done everything they could but now we had to just wait to see what was going to happen. I couldn't believe it. What a very long day and now for a very long night. John and I were very exhausted but were very nervous to leave Caleb, so we stayed right by his side. Because we didn't know exactly what was going to happen. At Stanford they have parent rooms, so John and I took turns sleeping.

We got thru the night, but Caleb was a very sick little boy. We met a wonderful family from Alaska. Their child needed a heart transplant and they were there until this could happen. We all tried our best to comfort one another on our journey. We had also met another family the time before that had happened to be there at the same time. Also, our friends we had met on our very first visit from Florida were there as well. I just thought it was so ironic that we all ended up there at the same time.

The next day Caleb's lungs weren't doing so well after the hit his heart took right after surgery. His lungs weren't too sure what to do with all the new blood flow. Caleb had a reperfusion injury. Basically, what this is, is with all the new blood flow the body gives off a signal that it is sick almost like a pneumonia. Caleb started running a fever because of this, so now they were very concerned. They started Caleb on a very high-powered antibiotic which is very harsh on the kidneys. After Caleb's code his numbers were kind of all over the place. Anytime you have a heart injury happen it usually affects the kidneys and now we're adding harsh antibiotics. I was so afraid. Caleb needed a miracle.

Days passed, and Caleb's lungs weren't clearing up. The doctor's thought that the shunt Dr. H had placed was too big and that Caleb wasn't able to handle it. They ran some tests and discovered Caleb had a very serious infection called pseudomonas. It is very dangerous in little children like Caleb. If not taken care of it could potentially kill my son. They thought that's why Caleb couldn't move forward and get off the vent. This trip was turning into a nightmare.

That night Caleb even being as sedated as he was still had wandering hands. Caleb found his way to that line and pulled it out half way. Then the next day he pulled it the rest of the way out. They had routine test that they ran on Caleb just to keep an eye on things. They ran a test that showed Caleb was now also positive for enterococcus. This is a bacteria that we all carry on our skin. The doctor wasn't sure and questioned the results thinking that maybe the test got contaminated. They ran the test again and sure enough Caleb had enterococcus in his blood-stream. He got it from when he pulled the line out of his liver. Now not only did Caleb have pseudomonas he also had entero-coccus in his bloodstream. Caleb was very ill and on the edge of death. His kidneys had now taken a hit and he was in renal dysfunction. Caleb was now closer to death then he had ever been. The doctors were very concerned and were doing all they could to help him to get better. Caleb was so sick, and I was having a hard time handling all this.

Caleb was still having a hard time getting better and now he was withdrawing from all the narcotics. His lungs were still a mess, but his kidney function was getting better. Caleb still couldn't get off the vent. Caleb had now taken a turn for the worse, he started peeing blood. They got him ready and rushed him into the cath lab to see if they closed off the shunt if that would help him. The doctors were very concerned sending him in but knew he needed to go. The doctors had the crash cart right in front of Caleb's room. I again was so terrified and was trying to hold it together. They went over everything with us and also explained that if Caleb coded in the OR that he couldn't be put on ecmo because his left lung was clotted off. (Ecmo Extracorporeal Membrane Oxygenation this is a machine that does all the work of the heart and lungs so that the patient's organs can rest). The doctor said that if Caleb coded they would try life saving measures for thirty minutes but it they were unsuccessful that they would stop. I had never been so afraid in my life. We prayed over Caleb and they took him away.

We went into the waiting area. There we were surrounded by friends. Even though they weren't our family they were there for us the whole entire time. It was crazy how God brought us all there at this time. I knew He did it so that we could all comfort one another as we went through our battles. We got our first update and they said Caleb was stable and doing very well. That was such a relief to hear. Another hour passed and the next thing we knew the doctors were right in front of us as they wheeled Caleb back into his room. He said Caleb did great and that he didn't need to close the shunt. He explained that in time Caleb should be ok. Praise God!

Days passed, and they were finally able to get Caleb off the vent. Caleb wasn't doing well, and we had been at the hospital for a few months now. John told me he was going to bring his girlfriend to the hospital. I was so upset. I couldn't believe that we were going through all of this and now he wanted to bring her! We got into a huge fight I said I don't want her here I haven't seen her ever and I didn't want to deal with her now especially during this time. He said she is coming and that's that. We talked to the social worker and there was nothing I could do, she was coming. I was so angry I couldn't believe that he would do that in a time like this.

The day came, and she arrived. I didn't know what to do or how to act so at first, I didn't say anything. It was time for Caleb to have his lungs worked on, so I asked her if she wanted to go? She of course said yes. Once we were in the room I know it was very overwhelming for her. Not only was Caleb very sick but the baby next door to us was very ill and transitioning into Heaven. The mother was crying with a wail I had never heard before in my life. It was soul crushing to hear that mother cry out like that. Once Caleb was done with his treatment we left to give the other family their privacy. She stayed two more days. It was very uncomfortable but if she was going to be in John's life she had to know all these things. If anything were to ever happen to me she would have to take my place and help John take care of Caleb.

Caleb was still not doing well but the doctor's all said there wasn't much they could do and that we should take Caleb home. I wasn't sure what they meant so I asked them directly. They said Caleb is a very sick little boy, his lungs are a mess, and his heart function isn't great. They said take Caleb home and cherish every day you have because Caleb isn't going to get better. My heart sunk!?! Was this really happening? Were they serious? This is it? I'm taking Caleb home to die? But this was the reality Caleb was sick and there was nothing more they could do. Heartbroken we prepared to take Caleb home. What a bittersweet day we had met so many people that I considered to be my family for life. We had been at Stanford for four and a half months. Watched thirteen children gain their angel wings during this visit and now they just told us that ours would soon be next. I couldn't believe it!

John decided he and Caleb were going to fly home because I had to head home early to get the house ready for Caleb. Luckily, I didn't have to drive all the way home I had Derane. When I got home all I could do was cry and just have a talk with God. I told God if he was ready to take Caleb home then it was ok if not just teach me how to make him better. I didn't want to see Caleb suffer, I knew I couldn't live life without him, but I couldn't be selfish. When John finally showed up with Caleb I hugged my little baby for what was probably hours. I was afraid that if I let him go I would never feel his warm embrace again.

God must have heard my prayers because slowly but surely, I saw signs of improvement. I was able to lower his medication doses. Caleb was on a very slow taper of methadone and Ativan to help take the edge off as he detoxed from all the narcotics he was on during that hospital stay. I was slowly able to wean him off his oxygen. Until I got down to a quarter liter and every time I would try and turn it completely off his heart rate would go up. I was concerned so I called Dr. H to explain the situation and he suggested we bring Caleb to see Dr. P, so she could do a heart catherization.

During the time it took for Dr. H to make all of the arrangements and referrals, Derane and I decided to get married. Even though Caleb was doing much better the reality was we weren't sure how much longer Caleb was going to be with us. We knew the ceremony had to include all the kids. I must say I truly feel that God had placed Derane in my life. The wedding was finally here, and it was beautiful. Ashley and Caleb walked me down the aisle and we had all our other children as our wedding party. I was so engulfed in love I just felt whole. Caleb had such a tough year I was so broken preparing for this birthday since it might be his last. Caleb really enjoyed the movie Cars, so I thought this year that would be the theme. I spared no expense if this was going to be his last it was going to be over the top. I got everything ordered even decided to get a jump house. I knew all the kids would love that

Today we will be celebrating Caleb's 6th birthday what a blessing. I was so thankful God allowed us to share one more year with Caleb. I can't lie it was heart wrenching each time I thought about it possibly being the last one but today Caleb was here, and we were going to celebrate. I decorated and set out the food. The men came and set up the bounce house just as they finished everyone started to arrive. It was so nice to see Caleb so happy.

The kids were so excited to see the jump house that was the first thing they all ran to. Caleb wanted to go in, but I was so afraid. His lungs were still pretty junky, and he was still on oxygen. I was hesitant, but Ashley reminded me that if anything were to happen at least Caleb should be enjoying himself. So, I reluctantly decided to let him go. He had such a  great time the smile in his face was priceless. Everyone stood around eating watching the kids run around having a great time.

It was time to sing what I just knew was going to be the last happy birthday. We all gathered around once we all began singing the look on Caleb's face was the face every mother lives for. I began crying I just couldn't help feeling like this was the last time. Caleb blew out the candles and we all cheered. He clapped with such enthusiasm what a great day everyone had such a great time especially Caleb. Happy 6th birthday son!

7

WISH

We had finally received the call from Dr.P that it was time for us
to head back up to Stanford. I couldn't help but think is this time
going to be the last time. We get there, and it was time for the
same routine. It was time for us to wait and pray. After some
time, Dr. P came to tell us that she found a collateral vein with
blue blood which was concerning. She told us that she coiled it
off and to take Caleb off oxygen completely. The surgery went so
well we were able to return home the very next day. While at
Stanford, I realized how sick he had become after his last surgery
and asked if it was possible that Caleb might be granted a Make
A Wish trip. The social worker at the hospital said that she would
put in the paperwork for him. A short time later, I got a call from
a woman named Amanda. She said she was with the Make A
Wish Foundation. She had called to tell me good news that
delighted my ears, as Caleb had indeed been awarded his Wish.
We scheduled the meeting where we would find out what Caleb
would like to do for his trip, what his one Wish would be.I was so
excited by the prospect of such a blessing being freely given to

my son. I so hoped that Caleb would be able to go when the time came.

After Caleb got out of the hospital, Derane and I decided that Caleb had earned himself a trip to somewhere special as a reward for all he had endured. Caleb loved monkeys, and if he didn't tell you so himself it became clear by the beaming smile stretching from one side of his handsome little face to the other as he tried his best to mimic what he had only seen on television. The stroke Caleb had suffered in his infancy made

curling both his arms under and scratching his armpits seemingly impossible, but one was enough when he coupled it with his best, high-pitched "Eeee! Eeee!" before the monkey sounds eventually gave way to laughter. I loved to see my son happy monkeying around at home, but we had the special trip in mind for the most deserving little monkey in the world and the San Diego Zoo would be the best place we could take him to see what he loved. We were right because Caleb could hardly contain his excitement as one by one he got to see all the different animals with his own eyes. He loved the variety of big and small, and the colorful as well as the camouflaged he sought so intently to see for himself. He especially loved the monkey exhibit. Derane and I had a great time, mostly just by watchingCaleb enjoy himself, and enjoy being a kid doing kid things outdoors in the temperate San Diego climate. It was a great getaway for each one of us and it would be a memory I knew Caleb would hold onto for his entire life. I loved to see Caleb experience life as much as he was able, but all the while I was deeply concerned by all the germs that he was being exposed to.

It was the day of our Make A Wish meeting. Once everyone arrived I explained to them that Caleb had suffered a stroke at such a young age and was therefore unable to communicate. I told them all each of the things he loved and enjoyed doing. Amanda listened intently and took notes. Once we had finished talking and had covered just about every detail imaginable, Amanda said the foundation would get in touch with me soon and that they would begin at once in putting Caleb's Wish together. I sighed a breath of relief and was grateful for what my son was having prepared solely for his enjoyment. LORD, what a great meeting that just occurred. Thank you for this blessing given to Caleb. With that, my mind began to wander, exactly where would they be sending Caleb that would or even could incorporate all the things he loved?

After a few weeks somewhat slowly passed by, I got the call from Amanda I had been expecting. She asked me to select a specific date, so they could in turn award Caleb his Wish. We set the date. The anticipation and excitement felt great. I was unsure what the Wish would entail so I wanted to guarantee that we had enough money to do whatever Caleb's heart desired for the duration of the trip. I knew Make A Wish gave you some spending money, but this was a once in a lifetime trip and with Caleb being so sick I wanted to be sure he could do everything. I decided to sell dinner plates to help raise money. I posted what I'd be selling each day, and seemingly all at once everyone began ordering. The fundraising was a great success and we sold them all around the Barstow area. My mom, daughter, niece, Marianne, and Derane helped me. The Barstow community was so excited to help. We raised quite a bit of money and I knew in my heart it was going to help make this trip even better for Caleb.

The day came when it was time for Caleb to be awarded his Wish. I invited friends, family, fire department, Mayor Joe

Gomez, police department, and anyone else that wanted to be a part of this very special day. I was so excited I could barely stand the wait. Amanda decorated the room at the Barstow Tot Time to be so cute. There was even a SpongeBob SquarePants cake and I orderedother goodies for all who attended. Once we were there Amanda and another representative from Make A Wish stood up and revealed to us what Caleb's wish would be. Amanda handed us tickets for a Southwest Airlines flight and said we would be going to Florida for a total of six days and five nights. She mentioned that we would be staying at the Nickelodeon Family Suites and that during our stay in Florida we would be going to both Disneyland World and Universal studios. We even received a check to cover some of the spending money while we were there…I began to cry and couldn't thank them enough. Then Mayor Joe Gomez had a surprise of his own: in his hand he had a certificate that stated the 19th day of June was now officially Caleb's Day in the City of Barstow. What a great day for Caleb. I thanked all the people for coming and we made our way home. We were all so overjoyed with all that had happened. We decided we wanted to remember this day forever so once we were finally home Ashley, Marianne, Erica, and I got promise tattooed on our pinky fingers to commentate this day. Caleb was always wanting to pinky promise so we decided that would be the fitting thing to always look upon and remember.

When the time came for us to go on our trip, A limousine came and picked us up right in front of our home. Wow! We were on our way. John had to work so he met us at the airport. I can't explain the excitement I felt knowing Caleb was about to have the time of his life, because of Caleb's delays even if I would have tried to explain it him he wouldn't have understood. So away we went!

Our flight was long, I was worried about Caleb because of his heart defect plus his low oxygen levels. I kept checking him every five minutes to make sure he was breathing normally. One check-up on my son was the last one before we were instructed to prepare for landing and a few minutes later we finally made it to Florida. We grabbed our checked bags from the carousel, carried all our stuff over to the car rental area, got the keys and loaded everything into the car and headed to the hotel. As we arrived, it was crystal clear that Caleb was so excited as he also realized that we were visiting a great place. He poured out all that excitement by looking around and pointing to all the different things he was seeing.

We checked in and were in amazement of the hotel. We took Caleb around the entire hotel to see everything it had to offer. It was so amazing to witness his Wish coming true. All the things Caleb loved were surrounding us in every direction: SpongeBob, Dora, and everything Nickelodeon had to offer. Next, we went out where the pool area was and couldn't believe our eyes! Their swimming pool was so big that Caleb wanted to get in that very moment, but it was getting late, so we went back to our rooms to get some rest. We knew the next few days were going to be jammed packed with so much excitement. Caleb fell right to sleep but I could not, I was so excited for what the next few days were going to be like for him that if my sleep was to be a casualty of this Wish so be it. Caleb was being loved unconditionally and whole-heartedly by Make A Wish and that made me so, so happy. And to think that it was only the end of a travel day, not even day one yet.

The next day we were up bright and early getting ready to eat breakfast. We went down to the restaurant and found out that a meet and greet had been arranged. As we were eating the various Nickelodeon characters would come out and dance around right in front of us. Once they were done they came to each table to hug and take pictures with the children. The look on Caleb's face was priceless! He wasn't sure what to do but the smile on his face said it all. Caleb was so excited to meet with Dora and Sponge-Bob. He was so beside himself. I'm sure in his mind he probably couldn't believe that he actually was right in front of them. He was on top of the world, on his own version of cloud nine, and he had not even finished breakfast yet.

We stayed at the hotel that day and rented a bungalow so that if Caleb got sleepy he could easily rest inside. We were having such a great time, which may sound repetitious but so far Caleb's Wish was repeatedly raising the bar on once-in-a-lifetime experiences. At noon they had arranged for Caleb to have his own special meeting, a VIP Meet and Greet with SpongeBob and Squidward. Caleb seemed a little nervous at first but within seconds he had warmed right up to them and by its end he and two of his favorite fictional cartoons-come-to-life had a real, memorable time together that I could see from the look on his face was to be a lifelong memory and cherished experience. We took so many pictures there. We wanted to be sure we didn't miss a single moment.

Once the meeting was over we headed back to the pool. Caleb played in the water and had so much fun. Every hour they would come out, play the song Everyday I'm Shuffling, and then proceed to dance around us. Caleb thought it was great and at the end of the song they would count backwards from ten and then dump a big bucket full of green slime on the kids. He did not like that, but he did not need to, he only needed to experience that once, which he did. We were so fortunate to have such a great first day. It was uplifting to continuously be front row and center and seeing your son enjoy life like he had no cares in the world. Now it was time to eat dinner and head off to bed. And with that day one was in the books.

The next day we were up early and ready to eat breakfast. We went down to the hotel restaurant again because Caleb had enjoyed it so much. He had a great breakfast for the second straight morning and then we were quickly rushing off to Universal Studios. What a great experience for Caleb that turned out to be. Caleb was so excited to see all the different things the theme park had to offer him that were visually amazing and stimulating to his curious mind, there was so much to look at it must have been overwhelming. So once more, we took lots of pictures and attempted to capture each moment I wouldn't want to miss for the world. While we were still inside the park we had the pleasure of meeting up with some of the workers who were working in the background with the foundation and making Caleb's Wish a reality. They had arranged a meeting so that Caleb would have the opportunity to meet Dora the Explorer.

But first, Universal Studios hosted a parade with all the characters on a float. Afterwards, we were able to take Caleb over and we met with all the characters. He was so excited all he kept screaming was "Mama! Monkey!" Monkeys were his favorite, much  more so after his visit to the San Diego Zoo earlier. Caleb screamed "Mama! Dora!" when he saw her, and he genuinely had love for the characters standing before him. Caleb was so excited to be able to go up to them and hug them. Once again, Caleb had an ear-to-ear grin on his face. I started to cry, Oh God thank you, it was pure joy to see my little man so happy! My heart was so moved by these simple interactions my son was having because most of the time Caleb was unable to experience even the simple things that a healthy person may take for granted! What a great day Caleb had. However, it was also a very long day and Caleb wasn't used to having that much activity. We decided it for the best to get headed back to the hotel. I gave

Caleb a bath and once he laid down he was knocked out cold in seconds flat. We settled in for the evening, fully cognizant that we needed to get plenty of rest because the next day we were heading to Disney World.

We got up early again and headed down to our usual place to eat breakfast. Caleb loved all the characters being there, even for a third straight morning. After we were done eating breakfast we headed over to the Magical Kingdom. To see Caleb's face in awe, as we were driving up towards the entrance, made me get all teared up and  emotional. I was in just as much awe as he was, the scale of this place was impressive. Disney World was so big it even had its own gas stations. We decided to go to the Animal Kingdom first because we knew very well all about Caleb's love for monkeys. So, the first ride we went on was like an actual safari. That was so cool to watch the animals running around free. Caleb really enjoyed seeing them in a more comfortable environment.

Once that was over we made our way over to see all the other exhibits, again with the monkeys being number one on our list. Once we had seen all the things at the Animal Kingdom we made our way over to Disney World. Caleb was so excited to see all the different attractions. We went on so many different rides, not all of them but enough of them and too many to keep track of enjoying himself. We wanted to get back to the hotel for dinner, mainly because it was Italian night and that's when the Teenage Mutant Ninja Turtles would be there. Caleb loved those guys.

We were sitting at the table eating dinner when the theme song for the Ninja Turtles started to play.

Caleb's eyes got so big and immediately he began looking around. That is when the doors opened and one by one and they all made their way out. Caleb could hardly believe what he was seeing. He kept looking at me and John yelling "Mom!

Turtles"! Caleb was so ecstatic! He was trying to get out of his chair because he wanted to see them so bad. Once they were done Caleb got his chance to spend time with them one by one. He kept hugging them and giving them knuckles. I know I'm a cry baby, but I was so happy to see my baby so happy. After dinner we went back to our room cleaned up and went to sleep. We had another big day in front on us tomorrow.

We got up like we had for the past few days went down and had breakfast. Caleb loved seeing all the characters, it really never seemed to get old for him. Today we would be heading to Sea World. That's what I used

some of the money we raised beforehand for. Sea World was not included in Caleb's wish, however he really enjoyed seeing all the sea life. We went to all the different shows. We also took him to all the places, so he could see and touch all the animals. Caleb was kind of grossed out, but I insisted he still touch them, and he did. We spent the good part of the day there but left early to drive around and see the different sites located in Orlando. We found a great spot for dinner called Boston Lobster Feast that featured amazing seafood. After our stop for food, we drove around for a bit longer and, of course, Caleb fell asleep -- this trip was taking its toll on him. He already had so many great days and we still had one more tomorrow. We were headed back to

Universal Studios. We got home, what we called our hotel after three nights, got cleaned up and headed for bed.

The next morning, we were up early and ready for our last day and last adventure in Universal Studios.Make A Wish had once again set up some meet and greets for Caleb. But first they had the Hop movie parade. Caleb was very excited to see some of the characters. Once we got up to them and it was our turn to take pictures, seemingly out of nowhere Caleb got this funny look on his face and then proceeded to have a total meltdown. Caleb didn't like Hop at all, he made that extremely clear. We had to get him away from them, we didn't want Caleb to start holding his breath because that truly could have put a bad twist on this great adventure.

After the bad Hop encounter, we explored the park again and took Caleb on a few rides.It was so amazing to see him enjoying life like a normal child, but still a worrisome thought lingered in the back of my mind, the truth being that I  was still concerned about germs. We headed back early so Caleb could share his last night with the Ninja Turtles. Once again, Caleb was amazed by them and was so excited just to be around them. As we sat there eating, I started to get emotional because I knew this was to be our last night at our Florida "home" and we would have to go back to our normal life soon and very soon. I tried to suck it up, as in that moment Caleb was enjoying himself and deservedly so. After dinner we headed back to our room. We got cleaned up, I gave Caleb his night meds, and I gladly patted him to sleep. After he was asleep, I packed up all our thingsas our trip was at its end.I was so sad to see it end as I wished everyday could be like these for Caleb.

The next morning, we went to eat our last breakfast at the

hotel. Caleb was very excited once again. While we were eating I noticed John was crying. I asked him what was wrong. He said he was sad that all this had to end, and it was his wish that everyday could be like this for Caleb, who as much as he had been through in his short life he was most definitely deserving of it! That made me get all emotional too! We agreed word for word that Caleb carried a burden deserving of a lofty reward, like living in this Make A Wish Nickelodeon dreamland. After breakfast it was time to pack up our car and head to the airport. It was a long flight home, but that gave us all time to reflect on the amazing trip we were all but done with, as home approached. Caleb had the time of his life. Once we were back the limousine was there waiting to take Caleb and I home. What a great way to end such a special trip.

Once I arrived home Derane was very distant from me. I knew the life with me was taking a toll on him. We weren't seeing eye to eye anymore and our relationship was starting to reach it's breaking point. And as much as I hated it, it was time for us to part ways. We decided to seek counseling as we lived separate trying to put things in perspective. Caleb was still my number one and I had to be honest with myself I didn't have time for much else.

Caleb started school but not the way other children did. Since his immune system was compromised he wasn't allowed to attend a traditional public school. Caleb had a teacher that would come to our home to teach him. In the California school district, it was called a Home Hospital Teacher. The first teacher wasn't really sure how to help Caleb, so I was referred to a woman named Ms. Mosel, she was the special needs teacher at Cameron Elementary school. I went down to the school myself to personally beg Ms. Mosel to be Caleb's teacher. I explained to her the severity of Caleb's medical history. I told her how he had suffered a stroke at the age of four so taking him on was not going to an easy task, but he really needed someone like her to help him. Ms. Mosel was enthused and said she is willing to take on the challenge. I was so grateful and couldn't wait for her to start. Her first day was awesome, Caleb was very excited to meet her. She showed up with a suitcase full of goodies and Caleb was ready to see what surprises she had in store. They were only seeing each other for an hour and a half every day, so at his next IEP I insisted on more. They added physical therapy, speech, behavior specialist and, OT.

As Caleb grew we realized the living room was not working anymore. My sister Cindi and I were talking and thought maybe we could convert the garage into a classroom. That way Caleb could have more room with less interruptions. My sister suggested that I talk to home depot because they are the ones who do Habitat for Humanities. I told her I would try and just see what happens. I made an appointment with the manager and presented the idea of a virtual classroom for Caleb. I thought if they could use social media to keep in contact why wouldn't we use the same concept for Caleb to go to school. I knew skype would be perfect for this. He was delighted with the idea and said he would contact his corporate office and see what they thought. I was very hopeful.

Just a few days later I received a call and sure enough they were excited to have the opportunity. They gave me a list of everything I would need to start the classroom. I ran things over with my mom and she said go for it. I was headed to the city hall and started the permit. I was glad Caleb would finally have a place where he could learn and flourish. The Home Depot sent someone over to draw up blueprints, a representative from the city came to overlook the garage and said there weren't any problems, so he would get the paperwork processed right away. That's when all the trouble started. I'm not sure how but the others who owned the house found out about what we were proposing to do with the garage. I never once thought they would have a problem with us doing this for Caleb. I received a call from the city and they informed me that they had put a stop to everything pertaining to the classroom. I made several attempts to call them and discuss the matter, but to my surprise I got no response. I was so hurt that all this was happening how could they do this to Caleb, after all they are my family! All I was trying to do was give Caleb the best life and still keep him safe from the outside world.

The very next day I was delivered a certified cease and desist letter from them preventing me from making any changes to the house. I was utterly shocked and embarrassed to have to go tell Home Depot that because of the other owners of the property, we would no longer be moving forward with the project. I reached out to numerous agencies just to see if there was anything else I could do but there wasn't. I even went to the local paper and started a petition to get people's attention. A few stories went out, but it wasn't impactful enough, so I started up a Facebook page called Fight for Caleb's classroom, hoping to get more attention and try and change their minds. Still no one seemed to reach out to me.

I informed one of them because they wouldn't respond to me I was going to come up to their church and speak with their priest about what was going on. I wrote "Fight for Caleb's Classroom" all over my car and wore a hot pink shirt that said the same. I was set up across from the church and was asking for help. I told a local reporter to meet me there since I was unsure of what was going to happen. It was really like an adrenaline rush I had never protested before. While there I was approached by several different individuals some who were pleasant others not so much. Finally, I met with the priest who said he knew them very well and would try and work with me to resolve the issue. After a while the reporter and I left, and I remained hopeful. I received a few calls from family members who were upset about the way I handled things. I kindly stated that I love them, but it was between me and them.

I wasn't going to let anything stop me from having that

virtual classroom. I had a bake sale in front of my house it was a real community event. I was shocked at how big of a turn out it actually was. Friend, police and the fire department all showed up to show support. Caleb even got to go for a ride in the fire truck. The bake sale ended up bringing in $300. The very next transformation to the room could begin!

I bought all the things we needed to start Caleb's classroom. Although Derane and I were no longer together we still remained friends. Caleb and Derane had a very unique relationship and we didn't want the fact that we were not together to come between that. Derane and I began to paint and of course Caleb wanted to help. We had to wait two days to make sure the paint was completely dry. In the meantime, I was searching Pinterest looking for cool ideas. I wanted it to have the feel and look as other classrooms would at the beginning of school. I filled it with ABC's, numbers, and all sorts of learning posters and things. It had taken some time, but I had finally done it, I got Caleb out of the living room and into a classroom.

The doctors up in Stanford hadn't seen Caleb in a while and they wanted to check up on him and see how his heart and veins were doing. John, Caleb and I headed up there, so they could do Caleb's heart catheterization. We went to our usual place and said a prayer. After three excruciating hours the doctor came out and said he had great news. He told us Caleb's veins were developing nicely. They went on to say that his heart function was doing much better since the last time they had seen him. Caleb had to stay overnight just for observation after that we made our way back home.

The first day of school officially began where Caleb could actually skype into class and meet all the other students. I was so excited for my baby that he could finally be a part of a real class and he could also be safe from all the germs. The teacher had made a chart with all the children's pictures, so Caleb could know exactly who each student was. One by one they all came to the computer and introduced themselves. Caleb was so overjoyed he was able to participate in circle time where they sang songs and read stories. It was really a sight to see. I couldn't wait to see how this was going to help Caleb in the future.

A few weeks later I received a call from Caleb's school saying Kaplow, the public relations company had contacted them trying to get ahold of me. They gave me the number so that I could contact a woman named Lauren and tell her all about Caleb's classroom. I was so excited I called her right away. Lauren was very kind as she listened to Caleb's history intently, I couldn't help but get emotional. She asked me if it was okay if she sent a reporter over to write a story, I told that would be awesome and I thanked her and hung up the phone. I just could not believe all this was happening, I was thrilled thinking about all of the children who would be able to benefit from this.

What a year we had it was a roller coaster. I was so thankful that Caleb received his wish and very devastated that family could be so mean and stop Caleb from having a classroom. In spite their efforts we still found a way around it and Caleb still got his classroom just in a room and not the garage.

Now it was time to start preparing for Caleb's seventh birthday. It had to be perfect. Caleb loved Ninja Turtles so that was going to be the theme for this party. I looked everywhere but there wasn't much I could find. I had to be creative and come up with the decorations myself. The only thing I found was a Ninja Turtle piñata.

It was Caleb's seventh birthday celebration. I decorated and prepared everything so that it would be a time to remember. It was time and now the guests started to arrive. Caleb was ecstatic to see everyone. It was such a great time. Everyone was enjoying one another's company. Kids were running around and playing games. I went in the house to get the cake I had made especially for Caleb. Everyone loved it! We all gathered around and began to sing. There was that smile on Caleb's face once everyone began to sing. I got a little emotional and was very thankful that after all that he had been through I was actually blessed to spend another birthday with Caleb. Caleb blew out the candles and everyone cheered. So much love filled the air as we celebrated one more year with such a special little boy. Happy seventh birthday son!

8

MISSION

Caleb was playing and ran into the kitchen where I was. He had footsie pajamas on and he tried to stop his momentum but couldn't and slipped. Caleb ended up falling backwards and hitting his head. He cried so hard that he was beginning to turn blue. He simply couldn't catch his breath. I went to him out of instinct and picked him up attempting to calm my little boy down before a bad situation escalated into something much worse it was scary to even give another thought to the real possibility I might be forced to if I could not calm Caleb's current panic. I called out loudly to my daughter and instructed her to dial 911. I knew Caleb was currently on blood thinners and was all too aware that this fall could be extremely dangerous for him.

The paramedics were swift and arrived on the scene, our own scary little scene; in less than five minutes! They all knew once our address popped up on their screens that it was Caleb in trouble and, thank God, they always responded very quickly. For children like my little Caleb, mere seconds often matter, and many times have been the difference between life and death. By the time they were there Caleb had calmed down, but a huge knot on his head remained. They transported us to the hospital, so they could run a certain test to make sure he didn't have a brain bleed, a risk those blood thinning agents circulating throughout his body only made more likely. I called

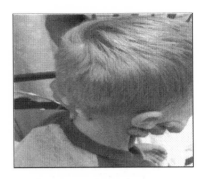

John while on the way to the hospital and he asked me to keep him updated on what was going on with Caleb. Once we arrived everyone sprang into action. They all knew Caleb and how complicated he was. They ordered an X-ray stat. Then they ordered a MRI. The results came back quickly. The doctor came in and said it looks as if Caleb has a small brain bleed and that they would be calling Loma Linda. They decided they would be transferring Caleb and wanted to know the best way to get him there where he wouldn't be in any harm. By now I'm panicking, and I wanted him airlifted. The doctor's explained that the elevation could increase the bleeding in Caleb's brain. I was upset and trying hard to keep myself together. I knew if Caleb saw me upset he would get upset and that could make things worse. They got ahold of the doctor and decided the best way to transport Caleb down to Loma Linda was by ambulance. Loma Linda said they would send the ambulance because they would have a cardiac team on board just in case Caleb had any type of event on the drive there. We waited and waited. I knew it wasn't a far drive, but I was worried, they had just told me that Caleb had a bleed in his brain.

By the time they got there Caleb's knot was the size of a bouncy ball. My nerves were shot I just wanted Caleb to get to the hospital, so they could fix him. I knew we weren't allowed to ride down there with him. I had already asked Ashley while we were waiting if she could get my bag packed and, in the car, ready for me to head down to Loma Linda as soon as we were done there. I always have a bag ready by the side of my bed so all she had to do was add a few things and I'd be ready to go. My sister was at the hospital so as soon as they had Caleb loaded up in the ambulance she took me to my house and I hoped in my car. I headed to the hospital I couldn't get there fast enough. On the ride there, so many thoughts were running through my mind. Some good and some very bad. I couldn't stop crying. I was praying and crying out to the Lord please save my son. I just couldn't bear the thought of losing him.

Once I got there I rushed into the ER. I called John and he met me there. Caleb was there already. The nurse took us back to him right away. When we got into the room he was watching SpongeBob. Caleb saw us and said mom SpongeBob. I started laughing and gave him the biggest hug and kiss. My son was such a little soldier! They were running test and decided to do another MRI. The doctor ordered stat on all the tests. They came in and told us there was no brain bleed. I was so happy and what a relief! Praise God. They decided to keep Caleb overnight for observation. I was happy they decided to keep Caleb just in case something changed they would be there. We settled in for the night, but as you know you don't get much sleep when you're in the hospital. I was just so relieved that Caleb was safe. All night I kept praising God for answered prayers and having mercy on Caleb.

We got up the next morning ate breakfast and waited for the doctors to round. Once they came in and checked Caleb they decided he was ok. They told us that they would get the paperwork ready and that Caleb could go home. What great news. The nurse brought the papers to sign. We loaded Caleb in the car and headed home.

About a month or so later Lauren from Kaplow set up the interview for Caleb's virtual classroom. She told me Beau Yarbrough from the San Bernardino Sun would be doing the interview. Lauren told me he was the educational reporter and was very excited to write this article. This was awesome. I thanked Lauren for everything. Once we were off the phone I was curious about the reporter. I went on the internet and looked him up. Beau had been a reporter for years He even traveled abroad reporting. I was in awe of all that I found out about him. I couldn't wait to meet him. Just as I was done reading up on him I received a call and it was Beau. We set up the interview. I thanked him and told him I was so excited to meet him.

Beau came and did the interview. It was great to finally meet him. Caleb was so happy to meet him. He kept telling Beau hi and giving him knuckles. Beau brought a photographer who snapped hundreds of pictures. Probably not that many but he was trying to capture that moment.

I wanted to send skype a thank you for everything they had done for Caleb and his virtual classroom. I wasn't sure how to do that. Then the saying "A picture is worth a thousand words" came to me. I knew now what I was going to do. I was going to take a picture of Caleb holding a sign like a photo thank you card. I didn't know what to write on it. I knew it had to have the Skype logo, so I printed it out. But I wasn't sure what I was going to write. I reached out to my dear friend Halima and told her what I was thinking about. Halima has always been good at coming up with catchy sayings, so I knew she would come up with the perfect thing. As we were catching up on things her mind was working I knew her creative wheels were turning. She was going on about Caleb being able to Skype into school and how it was opening up so many doors for him. Halima said how there was no limit on what he could do from home but at the same time be safe away from the germs. Halima said I got it " The Skype's (skies) The Limit For Me Now"! We both got so excited! It was perfect. I thanked her so much and told her ' You're the best." I hung up and got the thank you sign ready. I had Caleb put his signature on it.

I got Caleb dressed and ready for the picture. It wasn't easy. Caleb wouldn't stand still let alone hold the card. Getting the picture was almost impossible. After several tries I finally got the picture. It was so cute I couldn't wait to send it to her. I emailed the picture to Lauren. I'm not kidding in less than an hour I received a phone call. It was Lauren. She said that Skype loved the picture. They wanted to know if they could use that picture and post on their Facebook page. Wow! I said it was fine with me! Lauren said she would be sending over an email with a consent form I needed to sign giving Skype permission to post the picture. We hung up and I called Halima right away. Since she came up with the saying I wanted to ask her if it was ok before I signed anything. Halima was excited and said yes. I received the email signed the consent form and sent it back to Lauren. The next day the article Beau had written, and Caleb's picture were on Skype's Facebook page. People from all over the world were liking and commenting on the post. Skype even tweeted about Caleb's classroom on their twitter account. It was crazy but so very exciting. I couldn't believe that Caleb's virtual classroom was reaching people all over the world.

I decided to reach out to several television news stations explaining to them about Caleb's classroom. Everyone seemed intrigued but not enough to send out a crew. Then I spoke with Elaine at ABC and she was very excited. She said she was sending out a crew the very next day to film the story on Caleb's virtual classroom. I was kind of in shock that she said the very next day. I was having a hard time wrapping my mind around the fact that all this was happening. I was so excited as soon as I hung up I called the school district and talked to Superintendent Mr. Malan. I told him what Elaine had said and how excited she was. He was very excited as well. We both couldn't believe that this was happening but got on the ball. Mr. Malan got things together at the school and I got things together at home. I was so excited I could hardly sleep.

Today was the day. The ABC van drove up early. The came in and looked around the house and started setting up for the interview. I could hardly believe what was happening. Caleb was very excited to have company. He kept walking around saying hi to everyone and giving knuckles. It was time to film. We Skyped into Ms. Mosell's classroom like we did for school. We ran class just as we did every day.

After they were finished they gave hugs and said goodbye. Latisia told me it would be on the ABC evening news that evening. I said "Tonight?" She said "Yes tonight" and smiled. I was so excited. They headed down to the school to finish what they needed to complete the interview. I set the DVR and waited very anxiously for the interview. Everyone came over and we had dinner together. We couldn't wait to see it. The moment was here, and it finally came on. My heart was racing. As the interview played we all got teared up. They had done such a good job. It was so good. I kept pointing out to Caleb he was on TV, but he didn't really care he kept asking to watch Sponge Bob.

After all that, we settled back into our normal routine. Life had its ups and downs but that's just life. Caleb continued going to class and all the different teacher's coming to our home. Caleb was talking more and definitely learning more.

Babies So Special hadn't held a fundraiser in a while and I wanted to make sure we stayed active and had funds available to help disabled families. I thought a Walk-A-Thon would be a good idea. I began planning and getting this event together. I went to the schools and got the student's involved. I asked Mr. Delton who was the principle at the high school if it would be ok if we held it there. He agreed but we had to get the final approval from Mr. Malan the Barstow School Districts Superintendent.

I went to talk to him and He agreed it would be a great thing. We set up a contest and had prizes for the student that raised the most money could win. I reached out to the local businesses and told them what we were doing. They were happy to get involved. It was nice to see the event coming together.

The event was finally here. So many people showed up we had great turnout. John even came in support. It was time to start the event. The local Boy Scouts presented the colors and did the pledge of allegiance. Pastor John Perea (my Foster Dad) prayed. The Barstow Mayor Julie spoke, and the Walk-A-Thon began. The fire and police department even came and participated. After the walking part was complete I thanked everyone for coming, presented the awards, and everyone took lots of pictures. It was such an awesome event. It was great how our community came out and supported Babies So Special.

I was reading an article in the newspaper about a local child that was on the transplant list. As I read the story it talked about the strict requirements for the home of the transplant recipient. That when I found out you could not have a swamp cooler and qualify for a transplant. It can cause a mold and bacteria threat for the recipient due to the repressed immune system. The local child was on the transplant list and because her home didn't comply to the regulations she was removed from the list until the house was changed and an A/C was installed. I couldn't believe what I was reading. I knew Caleb would someday need a heart transplant I couldn't believe I never knew that.

I was nervous now because with a child like Caleb you never know when their health status could change, and they would need to be listed. I contacted the family members that were co-owners with my mother about changing the swamp cooler. I asked for only signatures on the permits to change the cooler to a/c. I received one letter asking for estimates. I got them right away. I sent them what was requested and never heard back. I just knew for sure this time there wouldn't be any problems because we were talking about Caleb's life now. The lack of response showed that there would be no authorization to change the cooler out.

I was so upset. I got on the phone and started making phone calls. I was trying to see what could be done because now you are talking about Caleb's life not a classroom. I reached out to the NAACP and the ACLU and they were unwilling to assist. They stated that this was a family issue. That was the craziest thing I had never heard anything like that in my whole life. I was horrified and very scared. What was I going to do?

My mom suggested that we reach out to the fair housing department. We called our local office and found out that because during the classroom stuff my mother decided to do a quick claim deed and put my name on the house in fear that those family members might try to remove Caleb and me. The women at the office told us there was nothing they could do it was a family issue. I thought not another dead end and begun to cry. She suggested we call an attorney. Ok then that's what I will do I told her.

I got on the web and started looking for attorneys that may be able to assist. I found one and made the first available appointment. My mother and I went to the office in San Bernardino, CA. In that meeting we found out that we could take action but that it could get all tied up in court for years. The lawyer explained that we would win but with Caleb being so fragile we didn't know how long Caleb had before he would need that new heart. He said the best thing was for Caleb and I to move out. I told him I didn't have means like that. We talked about other alternatives but said for Caleb's safety it was best for us to get our own home. The attorney said he would help me raise the funds needed to get Caleb out. This was so heartbreaking. After all Caleb had been through this was happening. On the way home, I was very upset and was thinking how I am going to raise money like that for a home. My mind was overwhelmed. I felt horrible that I couldn't provide something my son needed to prolong his life. My heart was broken, and I couldn't stop crying.

As soon as I got home I started thinking how I was going to raise money and be at home with Caleb. I thought well the one thing I'm good at and can do from home is cook.I had done that before with Caleb's Make A Wish Trip. I posted on Facebook that I would be selling dinner's soon to raise money for Caleb's Heart House. It was kind of embarrassing to let everyone know that I had to get Caleb out of the only home he ever knew. But I knew we needed to be free and I would do anything for my son to make sure he could have the best life.

I cooked five different times and raised $3,000 dollars. I thought ok if this keeps up I will have the money in no time to get Caleb the home he needed.Out of the blue I received a phone call from the City of Barstow. They asked me if I had been selling food out of my home? I explained that I had and what the money was for. The caller very kindly said there were regulations for things like that and that if I didn't have the proper licenses I would have to stop. I was blown away and started crying. I told the women I would stop. I hung up the phone so devastated. What was I going to do now? I had already talked to Caleb's dad and he said that I needed to do this with my own resources and that child support was all he was willing to do. I felt so sick. I started to panic and had an anxiety attack. I cried out (probably screamed) to the Lord what am I going to do now?

I tried to reach out to the attorney because I remembered what he had said about helping me and he never returned my calls. Again, I was at a dead end. My son is all I could think about. How was I going to make this happen? I thought I'll make Caleb Cakes and just ask for donations. I began making cakes. That brought in another $500. I thought ok not as much as the dinner's but at least I'm able to add money to Caleb's Heart Home Trust Fund. Then it happened I received a call from the San Bernardino County health department. It was the same questioning as the city. I explained that I was and why. Again, I started to cry. The employee on the phone said the same things as the city did. I needed to get licensed to be able to sell food out of the home. They even told me the person who reported me went as far as sending Caleb's Facebook link to show what I was doing. I asked the employee if I could know who reported me? They explained no it was confidential. I couldn't believe my ears. I was so devastated. How was I going to get this money together for Caleb's Heart Home now? I couldn't believe that someone would sink that low and stop a parent from doing what they needed to do to save their child's life! Then I thought who cared that much to go through all that trouble to stop me? I wasn't hurting anyone I was just trying to do what I could do to get the money I needed to get a home for Caleb.

I was so embarrassed and put a post out on Facebook that I would no longer be selling cakes. I asked everyone to please pray for me and asked if anyone had any ideas how I could continue to raise money? If they had other ideas to please let me know. I can't even put into words how I felt at that moment. I can say this as a parent I felt as if I had failed Caleb!

I was contacted by several people and we started doing different fund raisers to continue to build Caleb's Heart House fund. I was at Denny's and Jennifer asked if it would be ok if we did a fundraiser for Caleb there? I said of course. Then we hosted one at Chili's as well as IHOP.

We did a Zumba-a-thon. We raffled off many different things. I was contacted by Cardiff pool services and Dani asked if it would be ok if they did a raffle on a tiki bar? I said that would be amazing. I was so happy that all these different people and organizations were coming forward to help get Caleb's Heart Home. I received a message from a gentleman named Luis. He explained he had seen our story and wanted to donate a custom-made beach cruiser? I was so thankful. He sent me a picture and I posted it on Facebook. Caleb's school even got involved and had a dance to assist in the efforts to help raise money for Caleb's Heart Home. Caleb and his best friend Riley went. We treated it as a prom. Even people who didn't know my son now were coming out to help. Team Caleb Rocks!

I received a message via Facebook from a person named Angela. She explained that she had been following Caleb's story and that she had reached out to the Cadillac Ranch. Angela told me that she had spoken to the owner Allison about the situation and she had ok'd me to sell raffle tickets there for the beach cruiser. I had never heard of that bar, but I was so thankful for the opportunity! Angela said she would meet me there and help sell them. All I could do was thank her and think Team Caleb Rocks. I was feeling a little better that we would be able to raise the money and get Caleb's Heart Home.

The day was finally here, and I went to the Cadillac Ranch to sell the tickets. Once I was there, there was a bike run going on. I had never been to one of those. It was so exciting. I asked who Allison was and introduced myself. She told me to set up anywhere I wanted. I picked a table and set up. I brought a box with a picture of the beach cruiser and raffle tickets. As I was sitting there so many people were coming back from the run. The bar was filling up. It was a great group of people. I wasn't sure if people really knew what I was doing there since I had never been there before. I asked Allison if I could tell everyone about Caleb. She gladly agreed. I got up on the stage and began to tell Caleb's story and what had happened to us. With all eyes on me I got a little overwhelmed and started to cry. Allison took the mic from me and said bottom line guys we need to help her she has a very fragile child and needs to move from her current home. So many people came up to me giving me hugs and handing me money. I was so overwhelmed by the love these total strangers showed to me.And how they wanted to help us. They were all so kind.

I was approached by Hill Billy, Allison, Pat, and Paul. They were hugging me and saying how sorry they were that that was happening to us. They told me that they wanted to help raise more money and get us out of that house. They started brainstorming and came up with a date. They said they were going to have a poker run and car wash for Caleb. I was amazed that these total strangers had the biggest hearts and wanted to help us. I kept thanking them over and over again. I stayed a few more hours and sold tickets. When I got home and counted the money the wonderful people at the Ranch had helped me raise it was $1,100 dollars. I was in awe and very thankful for Angela (another total stranger) asking Allison for permission to sell raffle tickets from a customer cruiser bike Luis (another total stranger) had donated. God is so good and was blessing us so much. I knew again that #teamcaleb would be able to get Caleb his Heart Home.

The day was here for the poker run and the car wash. So

many people showed up to register. Also, so many people showed up to help wash cars. The bikes all lined up and it was time to head out. As the bikes revved their engines my heart was racing. The bikes were so loud I wished Caleb could be there to see all of that. He loved motorcycles. I knew he would have loved that. They all headed off for the run. While they were gone, we all set up all the things to be raffled, food, and the raffle tickets. After we were done setting up I went out and helped wash cars.

A few hours later the bikes started coming in. Now it was time for all the fun to begin. There were lots of raffles donated by so many. Allison started drawing the tickets and announcing the winners. The people were so excited. Allison had me come on stage to help. Hill Billy had won a corset and put it on. He started dancing around and people were tucking dollars everywhere. It was the funniest thing I had ever seen but the crowd loved it. The energy in that room was so amazing. These people had come out to support a child they didn't even know. These people were awesome.

That afternoon was so great. It was time to count the money and let everyone know how much was raised. Again, Allison had me come on stage. She said are you ready Cathyleen. I nodded yes. I couldn't speak I was over taken with too many emotions. Allison announce that they had raise $4,500 dollars. I started crying and hugged her so tight. I got the mic and was having a hard time getting my words out. Somehow, I did and saw so many people wailed up with tears even grown men. It was a very emotional moment for all of us. I was so thankful for all of them. I told them I loved them I knew Caleb and I had a new family.

As soon as I got off the stage I called John and asked him to bring Caleb for just a minute, so everyone could see in real life who they had all raised money for. At first John was hesitant but then agreed to bring Caleb. I waited for him.Caleb was finally there. I had someone announce that Caleb was coming in but for Caleb's safety if they could stay at a distance. I carried Caleb in he was so excited. He kept saying ready, ready. We took him on stage and everyone was so happy and excited to see him. Again, the tears started flowing. Now there was a very real little boy in front of them that they all realized he was very sick. It was a magical moment for all.

That's when Caleb met Marshall. He had been a part of the Ranch for a very long time. Marshall got brain cancer when he was 14 and beat it. Unfortunately, it had come back, and, in his thirties, he was battling it again. Caleb and Marshall bonded instantly. Caleb kept giving him knuckles and hugging him. They were all taking pictures. We took Caleb outside and Hill Billy let him sit on his bike. Hill Billy was so excited holding Caleb on his bike tears rolling down his face. He said to me what a privilege to meet and hold a special little boy. He said he would do everything in his power to make sure Caleb had all he needed. Hill Billy started the bike. Caleb's face lit up and he started laughing. It was sad, but it was time for Caleb to go. Everyone came outside, waved and blew him kisses. Caleb was smiling and waving back. Caleb was even blowing them kisses back at them laughing. What a great day. I went back in the ranch helped clean up. We all sat down and chatted. I thanked all of them for everything they had done and that we were even closer now to get Caleb his Heart Home.

I started actively looking for homes now. I contacted Mr. Courtney from HMS realty and the hunt began. We looked at several homes. We found one and put a bid in on it. It was perfect it had a/c and all appliances. It was very nice. Now we wait. I had no idea what went into buying a home, but I was quickly learning. I was blessed that had a great teacher. Mr. Courtney was such a God send.

I couldn't believe it in just a few days we got a response back. They accepted our offer. I couldn't believe that. That was so easy. All I could think was thank you Jesus we found Caleb's Heart Home. Ken started the process by having people come by to check things on the home. Everything was coming back great until we got the report from the bug guy. The add on the back had termites and the house had to be tented to make sure they all were dead. I wasn't sure how that would affect Caleb, so I contacted the doctor to see their thoughts. All doctor's agreed that it would be unsafe for Caleb because of all the chemical's. I was so sad, but I had to do what was best for him. I called Ken and told him that we had to resend our bid because of what the doctor's said. I was so sad. Why? Another let down. I thought we were so close, but I knew God had a plan and I had to trust Him. So back to the drawing board.

There were a few more fundraisers that were held while Mr. Courtney and I looked for homes. My best friend growing up Tera suggested we do a quarter panel auction. She explained to me exactly how to have one and we did. It was a fun time.Lots of people attended, and we added another $2,000 to Caleb heart Home Fund.

Mr. Courtney and I finally found a home. After five tries I didn't want to get my hopes up. When we walked in I knew this was the house. It would be perfect for Caleb. We put in the bid and waited. Mr. Courtney gave me a call a few days later and said that the offer was accepted and now we could move forward getting the house checked out. One check after another. They all came back good. I was so excited. Thishouse was going to be Caleb's Heart Home. I was so excited. All I could think was thank you Jesus! Now everything was accepted, and we were ready to sign the paperwork. I couldn't believe it was happening, but I was happy it was. Now all we had to do was wait for escrow to close and We would have Caleb's Heart Home.

This time we had a Birthday/fundraiser for Caleb. It was so exciting! We had bounce houses, games, face painting, raffles, bowling special, comedians, and so much other fun things going on. Caleb's birthday was circus theme. So many people from Barstow came out to celebrate

Caleb's 8th birthday with him. We even had a spot in the corner sectioned off so that Caleb could come and still be safe from the germs. Once Caleb was there everyone including Caleb was overjoyed. Everyone had a great time. That's when I learned that one of the students from STEM Academy Amber Woods came

up with the idea to sell feathers to help raise money for Caleb's Heart Home. Why feathers because their school mascot was the Phoenix. Mr. Hassle the principle presented all the money. How great was that, that the young lady came up with that idea to help a little boy she didn't even know. I was speechless. That definitely was a very emotional moment I couldn't believe what those children had done for Caleb.

It was time to sing happy birthday to Caleb. Everyone gathered around. Caleb kept saying ready, ready! Then everyone started to sing. Caleb was laughing and so happy. Once everyone was done singing Caleb blew out his candle's. He told everyone thank you and started blowing kisses. There wasn't a dry eye in the house. What a great birthday for Caleb. All the love that everyone showed to him was very overwhelming. It was time for Caleb to go. He had been out and around the germs a little longer then I would have liked but it was ok he had a blast. What a great day. Happy eighth birthday, son!

9

STRUGGLE

Escrow finally closed, and it was official Caleb's Heart house was ours. I was so excited! Mr. Courtney gave us the keys and said it's all yours! I started crying! After all the trials and hard work, it was finally happening. No more worries now we had a home for Caleb after he gets his heart transplant. What a relief! All that had to be done now was to move in and get the house ready. I couldn't even stand it I wanted to get out of that house and into Caleb's heart home, so no one could have control over what Caleb needed except me from here on out. I had been packing little by little. Everything was ready to go. Derane came and helped me move stuff in that same day. It was the greatest feeling ever! Team Caleb did it. We got Caleb his Heart Home! Praise God!

West Coast Heating and Cooling contacted me and told me that their company wanted to donate their services and install the air conditioning system that was needed on Caleb's Heart Home. I couldn't believe my ears! They had read the story in the paper and wanted to help. They wanted to be sure that when it came time for Caleb to be listed his home would be ready. I was so overwhelmed I couldn't even put into words how I was feeling. Thankful didn't describe what I was feeling. That was the one piece that troubled me because I wasn't sure how I was going to get it done. I had enough money for the house and had a little left over but installing an air conditioning system on the home we were moving into was going to be very expensive. The house was older and didn't even have any ducts. After talking with the owner, he assured me that they would take care of everything and not to worry they would make sure Caleb's Heart Home would be ready. Michael told me that he had been on the phone trying to get everything coordinated but wasn't sure if the distributor would be willing to donate the unit. I explained I had some money set aside and hopefully that would be enough to cover that cost. He said ok don't worry we will get that figured out. All I could do was thank him over and over again. What a relief Caleb's Heart Home would be complete and ready when it was time for Caleb to get his new heart. I hung up the phone in awe of the Lord. He had just provided the last piece of the puzzle. I could relax and enjoy life a little more now.

A few days later I received a call from Michael and he told me with great joy that the distributor had donated the unit. I started crying I couldn't believe what he was saying! So many had already done so much and now this! Wow! Michael went on to say remember how you were telling me about that park you wanted to build Caleb in the back yard? I replied yes! He said that money you were saving I want you to take it and buy whatever you need to turn the backyard into a park for a Caleb. I wish I could explain what that moment felt like, but I have no words to describe it. All I knew was my baby boy had the home he needed to get his new heart and now his very own park in the backyard. I got off the phone and was praising God because I knew it was all Him. I have never met such great people in my life! Team Caleb Rocks is all I could think!!!!

THAT EVENING I ordered the biggest swing set I could. I knew Caleb would be so excited when it was put together and he could finally wing (swing) in his own ark (park)! That's how Caleb would say it. The owner of the swing set company got it to us as soon as they could. Once I knew it was coming we setup the  date for anybody who wanted to come and help get Caleb's swing-set together. Once again Team Caleb came together. Marshall, Pat, Christy, Chris, Marshall's mom Denise, Montana, and many others came to help put the swing set together. We decided to BBQ. The day started out nice but as the evening set in it became very cold and windy. Marshall had had cancer for years now and had tumors in his lungs. I kept telling him it was ok that he could go but he refused he said he wasn't leaving until Caleb could swing. What a sweet man and the love he had for my son in just the few months he knew him was incredible! Marshall didn't leave until he had his swing set put together and he could see Caleb swing. The smile on Marshall's face was priceless. But more than Marshall's smile was Caleb's. Now he had his very own swing set in his Heart Home. Again, Team Caleb Rocks. They all loved Caleb so much and came together to give Caleb such a great gift. His very own park. I can't ever thank them for what they did for my son.

A few days later I got a call from Pat telling me that Marshall had to be hospitalized because the tumors in his lungs started bleeding because he chose to stay and finish Caleb's park. I was so crushed. I knew he was sick because of what he had done for Caleb! What an amazing man to sacrifice his health just to make sure my boy had joy in his life. Marshall was such a hero for sacrificing his life to make Caleb's dream come true! It was touch and go for a while for Marshall we almost lost him. But after lots and lots of prayers I am happy to report Marshall made it through and was finally released from the hospital.

I still had a shed that was at my Grandmother's home that needed to be moved to Caleb's Heart Home. So, a few guys got together and helped move it. Chris, Robert, Derane, Richard, and a few others helped me move it. After it was moved to the house a wonderful woman named Jennifer volunteered to paint Jake and the Neverland Pirates of the side of it to help make Caleb's Park even nicer. In just a few days she had the side painted and finished. I was amazed at her talent and how quickly she had gotten it done. Caleb loved it. There wasn't much shade in the back and if Caleb was going to be spending time back there we had to fix that. That's when Lloyd said if I got the stuff he'd build a gazebo off the shed. He and I went to Home Depot and that's what he did. Man, Caleb's Park was coming together so nicely. It was still missing something. While we were in Home Depot I showed the manager pictures of what we had been doing to Caleb's Heart Home. He said now that you have a home for Caleb what do you think if we come out and put the finishing touches on Caleb' Park? We want to do that for Caleb since we were unable to do the classroom. Wow! That was so great. Of course, I said yes and gave him a big hug thanking him. Now the wheels were turning to get Caleb's Park done. I couldn't believe it. God just kept amazing me with all the blessing He kept bringing to Caleb.

I received a call from my mother saying that my grandfather's truck was missing from her driveway. I knew it had to be my family member's doing. I found out they were at Barstow Tire and Brake. I decided at that time I would take Caleb down to meet them. I thought maybe this was the chance to resolve all that had gone on between us and that seeing Caleb might change their hearts. How could you look at that sweet face and not fall in love? My plan was to be quiet and at least let them have some quality time with Caleb. We walked in the building I introduced them. My heart was racing especially not knowing how that might go. Caleb was very excited and kept saying hi in his charming little way he did. He was so excited! I could not believe what happened next. They got up and walked straight passed my little boy and didn't say one word! I couldn't believe it. After all that had been done up until this point was cruel but to actually see him eye to eye and not utter a word. I was shocked. At least I gave an opportunity and tried to see if we could move past our problems. I was hurt for Caleb I didn't understand how a human being could treat another especially an innocent little boy that was way beyond me! I was a little hurt myself as I once looked up to them. I vowed that day that would be the very last time I would try to extend any more effort. I came to the conclusion it was their loss for not taking the opportunity to get to know such an amazing little boy.

The first Christmas in Caleb's Heart Home was very exciting. I was so excited. We all loved Christmas so much I couldn't wait to decorate. I had Caleb helping decorate the house. Caleb kept walking around saying ho,ho,ho. Christmas Eve came, and we set out cookies and milk for Santa. We watched the Grinch Caleb's favorite movie. I read Caleb the story of Jesus' birth and tucked him into bed. Once he was asleep Ashley and I set up all the stuff for Christmas morning. John came as soon as he got off of work Christmas morning. We both went in and woke Caleb up. Caleb wasn't too aware but made his way to the living room. He did that squeal like only he could do! Caleb was so excited to see all the gifts Santa had left for him! The joy and excitement on his face was priceless. I made breakfast for us. We all sat down and ate together. It was time for John and Caleb to have their time. He took Caleb for half of the day and then brought him back so that we could eat dinner with Caleb. Another great holiday with family and friends!

Caleb and I rang in the New Year together! Got all kinds of goodies to help us celebrate. Caleb really enjoyed the poppers! Anything to put a smile on my sweet boy's face. Of course, Caleb was knocked out by the time twelve got here but it was still a joy to have him snuggled next to me as the New Year rang in. I was so thankful to God for another year. After all the ups and downs from years past another year was such a blessing.

Caleb was becoming a young man himself. I had been noticing when men would come around Caleb he really enjoyed and needed that "guy time". He didn't have much of it. All his teachers were women and John's visitation was only 6 days a month. I decided to see if I could find a big brother for Caleb. I asked around on Facebook but unfortunately Barstow didn't have that program available. Also, because Caleb had to be in the house not too many people responded. I had a few tries, but it didn't last very long. I was discouraged that Barstow had limited programs and thought one day hopefully we can change that.

I found out that there was going to be a baseball camp in Barstow hosted by Dino Ebel. I was so excited I knew Caleb would love this. So, I signed him up to go. A few days before the camp Caleb got a runny nose I was so sad that if it didn't clear up he wouldn't be able to attend. Caleb had missed out on so many things in the past I was praying hard that he wouldn't have to miss this. The  day came, and his nose had cleared up. It was a chilly morning but to my surprise it warmed up and it was a beautiful day.

There were kids everywhere. Caleb had not been around many children and had horrible anxiety around them. The only children Caleb saw was when he Skyped into school, but they weren't close they were on a computer screen. Each person that signed up to teach the kids took individual time playing ball with Caleb. Dino Ebel and Aaron Sanchez Barstow natives really took to Caleb. It was nice that they stopped and did that for him. It was such a great day. Caleb had such a great time and I loved watching him enjoy a little normalcy.

Life was just moving Caleb was doing great. February is heart awareness month. On February 6th its national heart awareness day. I asked everyone if they could wear red in honor of all the children with heart defects. It was so great so many people wore red in support of Caleb. So many posted pictures in their red shirts. Crazy to think that 1 out of 100 babies is born with some kind of heart anomaly. I could only think how special I was to have one of those special babies. How much joy Caleb had brought to my life and so many others. The pictures people posted showed me how loved Caleb was. God had blessed me with such an amazing child.

I received a call from the Chamber and was notified that I was nominated for an award. It was for the up and coming volunteer. I had been nominated for the Walk-A-Thon Babies So Special had hosted. What an honor. The day came, and Ashley went with me. It was such a great event. I didn't win but my dear friend Robin Lard did. She definitely deserved it she does so much for the people in our community.

Ashley was very pregnant with my granddaughter Hannah. It was very hard to believe that I was going to be a grandmother. Ashley was living in Irvine going to school, but she decided with the baby coming it might be a good idea for her to move Back to Barstow. So right before her due date I went up there to help her pack all her stuff and move back. On March 30 Ashley and I went to the hospital for her stress check after we had a great lunch. It was her normal checkup but because Ashley had developed similar high blood pressure the doctor wanted to keep an eye on her and the baby.

They hooked her up to the machine to monitor the baby. Hannah wasn't moving much and every time she did her heart rate would drop. Ashley got stressed out and started having contractions. Doctor C came in and checked on her and order an ultrasound to see what 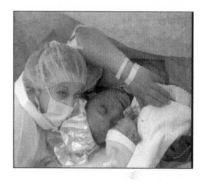 was going on. The doctor said he was going to keep Ashley and that he would induce labor the next day. Ashley went for her ultrasound. As soon as she got back the next thing we knew the nurses were rushing in the room prepping Ashley they said we must get your ready for an emergency C-section. Our hearts sunk. They told us the ultrasound showed that Hannah's umbilical cord was wrapped around her neck. I immediately got on the phone and called everyone. They got Ashley ready and I got ready. They wheeled her into the delivery room and as soon as she was in there and had her epidural in they had me come in. Dr. T and Dr. C were both scrubbing in. It was great to see them as they were the doctors for Caleb until we discovered Caleb had heart problems. Ashley was very nervous and very sedated all at the same time. She kept asking me if she was flying. It was so funny I kept replying Ashley you are not flying you are strapped to the table. She then kept asking me to check she was sure that her guts were spread all over the table. I kept reassuring her that they weren't and that the doctors knew exactly what they were doing. Finally, they got to Hannah. I could hear Dr. T counting one, two, and three. That's how many times her umbilical cord was wrapped around her neck and once around her shoulder. Thank God Hannah was fine under the circumstances.

Caleb was doing well and loved to play baseball, so I signed him up for T-ball. Caleb loved getting out of the house and of course playing ball. John and Caleb had been practicing and Caleb could hit the ball. At every game John would pitch to him and he could smash the ball pretty hard. He was so proud of himself. We would let Caleb run to first base but then I would pick him up and run the rest of the bases for him. It was way too much for him. When Caleb would get his turn to be out field he could care less about catching the ball. It was funny watching him. Caleb would get so impatient and sit down or run off. Caleb went on his first field trip with his class. Of course, Caleb couldn't go on the bus, but we followed them in my car. The class field trip was to Forever Wild Exotic Animal Sanctuary. Caleb was so excited to see all the different animals and to hang out with his other classmates. It was such a great time for Caleb. He definitely had a great time and that was another great moment in Caleb's life.

Caleb was done with the season and they had a party for the team. Caleb received a trophy and because it looked like a ball he threw it and broke it. It was kind of funny but sad all at the same time. But luckily, I was able to glue it back together. Caleb enjoyed the party because they hosted the party at John's incredible pizza. He loved it there. He didn't even want to eat he just wanted to play.

They had an end of the season trip to the Maverick stadium in Victorville, CA. Caleb and all his teammates went. We had pop up tents. All the parents brought food and we barbecued. The kids played together while the parents sat around and chatted. After we were done eating we took the kids into the game. They had fun watching and at the end they had all the kids come on the field and run the bases with their mascot Woolly Bully. After they were done they presented Caleb with one of the broken bats with some of the baseball players signature on it. Everyone was so excited to meet Caleb. One of the managers even got a ball and had all the players sign it and gave that to Caleb as well. John even let Woolly Bully sign Caleb's head with a Sharpie. Caleb again had such a great day. After that John took Caleb home with him and he got to go to the fair as well. I didn't go but John sent me pictures. What an amazing day for such a special little boy.

Marshall and Caleb stayed very close. We had got a call from Pat she told us Marshall had taken a turn for the worse and that he wanted to speak to Caleb. We called him. You could hear the joy in Marshall's voice hearing Caleb. He asked me if I could take a picture of Caleb because he wanted to see his face. I took a picture and sent it right away. Marshall said I love that little boy with all my heart and kept thanking me for allowing him to get to know such a special little boy. A few days later Marshall went home to be with the Lord. The Cancer had finally taken him after such a long fight for so many years. They asked me if it would be ok if Caleb rode on Hill Billy's Harley into Marshall's service. Of course, I said it would be an honor. I got t-shirts made with the picture of Caleb and Marshall in Caleb's ark. Marianne and I got Caleb ready. On the way when we were driving to the service that song "See You Again" played. Marianne and I started balling. Our hearts were so heavy we all loved Marshall so much. Once we got there Caleb was so excited to see everyone and all the Harley's.

He had no idea that he was getting ready to have his first ride for such a very special moment. Pat brought a helmet especially for Caleb. We got him ready for the ride. We sat him on the front with Hill Billy and Annette was behind holding Caleb with her hands wrapped around. They started revving up the Harley's getting ready to go. All you could hear was Caleb yelling mmmoooommmm as they rode off. It was so amazing. After they drove into the place with Marshall Annette told me all she could feel was Caleb's heart racing with excitement as he kept calling out for you. What a wonderful experience for Caleb. During the service Caleb started coughing really bad and I didn't have his inhaler, so we had to leave. All I kept thinking is farewell my friend I love you! Fly high with the angels you are free now!

The day came, and Home Depot was able to come to Caleb's Heart Home and finish Caleb's park. I invited everyone in the community to come and be a part of this great event. I came up with the idea to get paint and have everyone who attended put their handprints on the shed. So, we could always look at the shed and remember all the

helping hands that helped not only with getting Caleb's Heart Home but also helped with Caleb's park. We barbecued. So many people came by. Firemen, policemen, emt's, Mayor, and so many others. Of course, Caleb was so excited to see everyone and to be able to watch the backyard be transformed into a "ark". He smiled knowing everyone came to be a part of his special moment. Of course, Beau Yarbrough from the Sun came and wrote a story. It was so great to see him as well. There was so much laughter and tears as we all came together to finish Caleb's Park. To think that all these people loved my son and wanted to make sure that he had some normalcy in the world he was confined to. I couldn't thank everyone enough. I was so glad that I came up with the idea to put the handprints on the shed so that we could always look back and remember all the helping hands that helped make Caleb's life amazing.

I had started Fight for Caleb's classroom on Facebook in 2014. After we got the classroom I changed the name of Caleb's Facebook page to Caleb Lucas Incredible Heart Journey. In July 2015 Caleb's Facebook page hit 1000 followers. I was so taken by this. One thousand people were following my son's story and wanted to be a part of his life near and far. What another great moment in Caleb's Journey.

Caleb had to go for an echo at Loma Linda. Dr. G wanted to see if there were any changes. Marianne went with me and after we had decided we were going to take Caleb to John's Incredible Pizza. He loved going there and playing all the games. Caleb did very good at the visit. Dr. G said that Caleb's heart was holding strong and unchanged. We were all very happy with that. So, after the visit on our way home we stopped. Caleb was so excited he didn't want to eat. I got a little food in him and then we were off to go play the games. Caleb was going every-where and was very excited. There was a video game where you could ride a motorcycle. Of course, Caleb wanted to do that he loved motorcycles. I put him on there. He kept calling out to me mmmmmooooommmm. He was having so much fun. I love watching Caleb enjoy the things we see as simple but for Caleb it was so big compared to his very simple existence in his daily routine in his Heart Home. We let Caleb play for as long as we could but unfortunately it was time for us to go. As soon as we got home right into the bath he went to make sure we got all the germs off him. The day tired Caleb out so after the bath and his night medications we snuggled in for bed.

I had noticed that Caleb wasn't sleeping well. He fell asleep, but he couldn't stay asleep comfortably. After getting his echo and knowing his heart was ok I made an appointment with Dr. W who was his ENT Doctor. She was the one who had done the surgery and fixed Caleb paralyzed vocal cord. Dr. W put a scope down Caleb's nose and discovered his adenoids were swollen and thought that was the problem. She suggested that I do this nasal rinse and see if that would help. She said I'll see you in a few weeks to see if that clears it up. Dr. W even scheduled a sleep study just so that she could see exactly what I was talking about. I was relieved because I was very concerned about Caleb's body not being able to rest. I was concerned that it could affect him adversely.

It was time for Caleb's sleep study. Caleb is always so brave when he has to get these tests run on him. The technician got Caleb all hooked up to all the wire and probes that would help determine if there was anything going on while Caleb rested. Caleb drifted off to sleep but like always couldn't rest for long periods of time. I would always see him stop breathing and have to readjust himself. I was glad that he did it while he was being monitored. The morning came, and the test was completed. We headed home and now wait for the results. Later that day I received a call from Dr. W and she confirmed that indeed Caleb did have a mild case of obstructive and central sleep apnea. She suggested we remove his tonsils and adenoids and that should help him with his sleep. She said before the test though she wanted us to see the pulmonary doctor just to see how his lungs were doing and what that doctor would suggest to help what we had just discovered with the test.

I made all the appointments for Caleb so that we could see what the other doctor's thought about his current status. Caleb went to the pulmonary doctor and she said his lungs were doing great, but she suggested that we use oxygen at night when Caleb would sleep that way if his oxygen levels dropped that it wouldn't be hard for his body especially his heart to bring his oxygen saturations back up. I knew that Caleb would definitely hate that and fight me. Caleb had been on oxygen before and at times it was so hard to keep the tubes on him. I think somewhere in Caleb's mind that the tubes made him associate being sick. My little guy had already been through and fought through so much and now it felt we were taking steps back.

We also made an appointment with Dr. A to see how Caleb was doing neurologically. We went to the appointment and as always Dr. A was always happy to see Caleb and was astonished at all the progress he had made over the years. Dr. A was the doctor that had treated him when he had those seizures at four and half months old when all the damage was done to his brain. Caleb of course was very charming and telling everyone hi. Dr. A gave his ok for the removal of the adenoids and tonsils. So that was definitely a relief. Now all the doctors were in agreement that this was the best course of action for Caleb. I was hoping and praying that this would be the answer to help my baby to finally get some much-needed rest.

We were back into living life the best we could until Caleb could have his surgery. Ashley and I took Caleb to a baby shower for Ashley's best friend. I knew that flu season was coming quick and Caleb would be stuck back at home. It was a pool party and Caleb was very excited. Caleb loved the water. He actually stood at the side of the pool and jumped off into the pool. I was so proud of him but not as much as he was proud of himself. I was so happy that Caleb could enjoy himself. But because he wasn't getting enough rest just an outing like that really tired him out. So, we didn't stay long. Had to take Caleb home so his body could rest.

I was very concerned about Caleb not resting so I was staying on top of the doctor's, so we could get his surgery date and get those adenoids and tonsils out. I finally received a call and we got the date September 16. I was excited and scared all at the same time. I wasn't sure how this surgery would go for Caleb. Sedation is always dangerous for Caleb and then I wasn't sure how he would deal with pain like that. Plus, Caleb was already so thin, and I knew he probably wouldn't want to eat after that.

At that moment I couldn't stress over the what ifs I knew this was something that had to be done.

We took Caleb to Disney-land. Marianne, Ashley, John, Hannah, Erica, and I were so excited to be taking Caleb. He loved it there. We went on all the rides. They had added a Frozen play and of course we couldn't miss that. I knew Caleb would love to see all the charac-ters. Once in the room and the  show started Caleb's face lit up. He was smiling ear to ear! You could tell he couldn't believe by the expression on his face that the people he watched on tv everyday were actually right before his eyes. Caleb was so overjoyed. It was so awesome to see my babies face light up like that. The expression was priceless when snow fell on us. He was laughing so hard. We all got teared up to see Caleb so happy and enjoying himself. After the show was over we went and took pictures with the characters. Caleb was so overwhelmed to be standing in the presence of Anna, Elsa, and Olaf. After that we went and rode all the different rides. We took a break to eat but again Caleb was so excited to be at the happiest place on Earth he didn't eat much. As the evening fell we made our way over to the parade so we could have a good seat. We found a place that was perfect and before you knew it the parade started. Caleb again was so excited he was laughing and dancing around. He kept calling out to me and his sister! Ashley and I were so happy that Caleb was having the time of his life! The parade was over, and it was time to go. You could tell Caleb was very tired from the day's events. Once John got him in his truck Caleb was knocked out. I knew he would be, but it defi-nitely was worth it Caleb had an amazing day at a place he loved so much.

Lloyd was doing yard work in the backyard keeping Caleb's park clean and in order. There was a dead tree stump still buried in the dirt Lloyd asked me if he could take it out and of course I said go ahead. Once he pulled it out Lloyd thought it looked cool, so he put it in the corner and we decided to keep it. I had purchased some lights for the backyard so when the sun went down it would be lit up. Derane had stopped by to see it. As I took him to the back to see what was done we both noticed the tree. Derane said am I tripping or does those roots look like Jesus hanging on the cross? I said no it does. It was crazy that the dead tree roots would resemble Jesus on the cross. We went on to talk about that and it brought to mind that in the Bible it says to be rooted and grounded in the Lord. I knew at that time we were exactly where we were supposed to be. What a message God had brought in the roots of a dead tree that was in Caleb's Park. Amazing!

The time was coming very quickly for Caleb's surgery to remove his adenoids, tonsils, and put injections in his vocal cord. Anxiety was building up but at the same time I knew he needed them to be removed so my sweet boy could finally get the rest his body needed.

The day of the surgery was here, and we made our way to Loma Linda. Caleb was the first case. We walked with Caleb as we always did. We said a prayer over him and headed into the surgery room. John and I moved him to the table and helped hold him till he was gassed to sleep. We left the room and went to wait. The surgery was very quick within less than an hour he was done and heading back to recovery. Dr. W came out to talk to us and said the surgery was very successful. The doctor had his tonsils with her, so we could see how enlarged they were. I of course took a picture. They were huge! They kept Caleb overnight just because of all the past problems we had have over the years of him stopping breathing after anesthesia. Dr. W told me she had placed the NG tube during surgery and as soon as they felt like Caleb could tolerate it we would start feeding him.

Caleb did great and was starting to wake up. The doctor knew Caleb would be upset when he woke up and it would be best for John and I to be there. Caleb was sleeping nicely at first but as he started to wake up he got very agitated. I wasn't sure if he was in pain or from the anesthesia. They finally had Caleb's room ready in the CVICU. We headed up to the room with the staff. Caleb was in a lot of pain, but they thought Tylenol and Motrin would be enough.

The next day we went home. Caleb was having a hard time coping with the pain.Because he was delayed he didn't quite understand what was going on with him. I decided to take him to the Barstow ER. There the doctor's prescribed him Tylenol with codeine and sent us home. That worked a little but not enough to get his pain under control. The next day we headed to Loma Linda where they prescribed him Vicodin. They kept him over night until they could get his pain under control. All the pain was making his heart rate high and that was a big concern for all of us.The next day we seemed to have Caleb's pain under control, so we were able to go home. Once at home Caleb was resting but refused to eat. He wouldn't even swallow. Once we were home Stephanie brought Caleb a surprise to help make him feel better. Caleb was very happy to see someone else's face. My other friend Lisa brought Caleb tons of Frozen things trying to cheer him up. Lisa brought lollipops hoping he would lick one. Caleb had one in his hand saying ready but still wouldn't put anything in his mouth. Thank God for that NG tube or we would have been in trouble. The next few days I talked to the doctor and they said I needed to start trying to get Caleb to swallow that's what was making his recovery so hard. The nerves in his tissue was taking longer to heal because Caleb refused to swallow anything. I started putting stuff in syringes and had to force him to swallow it. It was such a fight, but I knew he needed it. I hated fighting him like that, but I had no choice. Finally, on the 26th he finally drank some ginger ale. We were so excited now we had finally turned the corner and Caleb was eating and drinking on his own. Unfortunately, because Caleb had so much Narcotics in the past he now was dependent on Vicodin. Now to start the wean off that. That I must admit was the hardest. Caleb had the most violent withdrawals. His body ached and the only thing that helped was putting him in the bathtub. Caleb also still wasn't sleeping well. I wasn't sure if it was the withdrawals, but I was keeping an eye on everything. I let the doctors know that Caleb was still struggling and not resting well. They instructed me to give it some time and if it persisted we would do another sleep study. My poor baby had been through so many things and now this. This surgery was supposed to make things better for him and right now things weren't better, they actually seemed worse. I hated watching my little boy suffer like that. I felt so helpless.

I was still getting things ready for Caleb's 9th Birthday party. Of course, it had to be Frozen! I had ordered an Olaf costume for Caleb to wear.

Kym Caleb's God-mother and I decided we would do a taco cart for the party. I had made so many different decorations. It was time to decorate the nice room with everything. There were balloons on the ceiling with snowflakes attached at the end of the string. I had lights everywhere. To top it off I even got a fog machine to give

it the Frozen feel. The kids and even the adults loved it.It was such a great day. Everyone started showing up to celebrate Caleb's ninth birthday. We had a bounce house. I even was able to find an Olaf piñata. We got Caleb dressed in his costume.

Caleb was so excited to be Olaf. It started to rain but that didn't stop us! We all were determined to make Caleb's day special. So many people showed up and celebrated with us. All the kids played in Caleb's park. The kids even played pin the nose on Olaf. It was great seeing Caleb and all who attended having such a great time. We played music and even Caleb was dancing around enjoying every moment.It was such a great feeling to see him enjoying life. Happy 9th birthday son!

10

FINALE

We had to take Caleb to Loma Linda because he wasn't feeling well. He was running a fever and his heart rate was elevated. They looked Caleb over and diagnosed him as having an ear infection. They prescribed him antibiotics and sent us home. Caleb still wasn't feeling good and not sleeping well either. I kept praying over him asking God to please give my baby a break. I just kept doing what I knew to do to help him feel better. Needless to say, during that time Caleb practically lived in the bathtub. That was the only thing that seemed to help ease his discomfort.

I had to do something to keep my mind at ease, so I decided Caleb's room had been Jake and the Neverland pirates long enough and needed a change. He loved Dr. Seuss so that seemed to be the perfect theme. I started looking for ideas and the transformation began shortly thereafter. It took some time, but his room was coming along nicely. I found lamps at thrift stores and covered them with materialthat matched the layout. The theme was Cat and the Hat and I made kites for thing one and thing two. I even ordered a sheet and comforter set to match. Caleb absolutely loved his room. It was like his own personal oasis getaway and the colors were amazing.

Caleb was coughing really badly, so I took him to the Barstow ER. They conducted some testing, did an x-ray and again prescribed antibiotics and sent us home. I just couldn't seem to keep Caleb from getting sick. My baby was just unable to catch a break. Unfortunately, on top off all of this, he still wasn't sleeping well. I was insanely stressed out and afraid that things would only get worse. I repeatedly called the doctor's in an attempt to determine what to do so that my precious son could get some much-needed rest. I even asked if we could do CPAP, but Dr. G said it would adversely affect the pressure within his Glenn. My level of concern intensified whereas I knew that if he was unable to get adequate rest that something bad was bound to happen.I was at my wits end and all I wanted for Caleb was for him to get a good night's rest. Oh,how the both of us so desperately needed sleep. I knew that I would be fine but was uncertain of the level of impact that the lack of sleep had on him. Dr. W finally ordered another sleep study, but itwouldn't be until December 22. Hopefully this study would help get some answers. It had only been a month since Caleb had his tonsils out and had been weaned off of the Vicodin. At this point I didn't know what else to do for my baby.

We were trying to make the best of everything. We prepared for Christmas by decorating the entire house. Of course, Caleb helped, he loved Christmas. I finally got Caleb's cough and cold to go away but he still wasn't sleeping well. December 22nd came, and it was the day for him to have his sleep study. John took Caleb this time and I kept asking him to send me pictures because it was the first study that I wasn't present for. They got Caleb hooked up and off to sleep he went. In the morning I asked John how Caleb slept, and his response was that he'd slept great. I was happy for that but later that afternoon the doctor called and said nothing had changed and that Caleb still had mild obstructive and central sleep apnea. I got very upsetand started to cry. Now what? I asked the doctor. How were we going to fix Caleb and how was he going to get adequate rest? He hadn't slept well for months now and I was very concerned that something was going to happen. Dr. W said let me consult with the other doctor's and we will figure something out. I was at an all-time low and extremely discouraged because I didn't know what to do. I felt like I was failing him as a mother. I cried out to God please help me make my baby well. All I wanted for himwasto be able to sleep peacefully.

For Christmas Eve everyone came over and we baked cookies and decorated them.It was so nice having everyone together as we listened to Christmas music. We were just enjoying each other's company.

As a tradition we let the kids open one present each.They were so excited to choose which one they would open. After-wards we all gathered around and read the night before Christmas. It was time to tuck the kids in,but before that we ensured that milk and cookies were left out for Santa to enjoy. Once they were asleep we neatly  arranged all of the presents. I couldn't wait for them to wake up and see the assortment of gifts. Iwasn't sure who would be more excited, us or them. That night we had an amazing time bond-ing, and everyone stayed the night at our house.

We all woke up to John knocking on the door. We waited for him to get off of work so that he could awaken Caleb. The antici-pation was bubbling over as to how Caleb would react to seeing what Santa had brought for him.Once John arrived he woke him up and everyone went into the living room to watch Caleb. He was so excited seeing all of the goodies. He was running all over the place and wasn't quite sure which one to start with. I went into the kitchen to make orange juice and cinnamon rolls. It was a family tradition that my grandmother had started years ago. I also made a quick breakfast and we all sat down to eat. Afterwards, John and I got Caleb ready and then off he went with John for half of the day. After their departure, we spent the next few hours preparing dishes and placing the final touches on the Christmas dinner. I got a call from John asking if he could bring Caleb back a little early because he wasn't doing too well there with all of the other kids. John said Caleb wouldn't calm down and was continuously crying. I was a little upset because it was Christmas day and wanted Caleb to spend time with his dad. Once Caleb returned we enjoyed the rest of our day with family and friends.It was another great day for Caleb. It made every momentof the struggle worth it to see him smiling and enjoying himself! He most definitely needed it after all he had been through over the past few months.

It was now New Year's Eve. Caleb and I always spent it together, but this year was different. Ashley and Hannah decided to come and bring in theNew Year with us. We ate dinner and watched TV. Afterwards we popped poppers and bonded while loving on one another. Caleb still wasn't sleeping well and became tired so we all cuddled up in the bed. I was so happy to have my family with me to bring in the New Year. As the New Year rang in Caleb was sleeping so Ashley and I wished each other a Happy New Year. Soon after we also fell asleep. As I dozed off I thought how great it was that we'dmade it to another year with Caleb still here. What a blessing!

I could tell Caleb wasn't feeling well. I put him in the bath hoping it would relax him and that maybe he'd get some rest. It allowed him to rest but when he woke up he wasn't looking too good, he looked somewhat purple. I gave him a breathing treatment, but it didn't seem to work at all. I dialed 911 and as always within moments, although it felt like an eternity, the fire truck had arrived. I called John and told him we were on our way to the hospital. While we were riding in the ambulance Caleb still wasn't breathing well so they administered another breathing treatment. His heart rate elevatedup to the150' andthey took his temperature which read 102°F. By the time we arrived at the hospital the treatments had kicked in and he was breathing much better. Thank God! Caleb's color was looking a lo tbetter. John arrived, and the doctors came in quickly to assess Caleb. After evaluating and doing x-rays they discovered that Caleb had a double ear infection which would mean another round of antibiotics for the kiddo. It was such a relief to receive an accurate diagnosis and now we could go home and try to get some rest. John followed us home to put Caleb in bed and then headed out. For some reason he never stayed and would always say to jus tkeep him posted. Of course, this frustrated me terribly but what could I do? I could do what I always did and that was to take care of Caleb the best way I could and help him to get better.

John picked up Caleb for their visit. Although Caleb was very happy to see his dad, I expressed my concerns with him about spending more time with Caleb. John would always get upset whenever I would bring up that particular subject. He would always reply, "I am doing the best I can." I explained that with all that had been going on and now that we were moving towards a transplant that we didn't know when things would change for Caleb. I told him that Caleb needed him to be around more than ever and that being a parent requires full-time commitment. John blew me off like always so in order to ease the tension I kissed Caleb and told him to be good for his dad.

I went into the house and got ready for the fundraiser taking place at the Cadillac Ranch. They had done so much for Caleb that I always made sure to help them whenever I had the opportunity. With the event off to an amazing start and everyone having a good time, it was looking to be a great day. That was up until my phone rang, and it was none other than John calling. I thought it was odd but from time to time he would call because Caleb wanted to talk or sometimes just to tell me about something funny Caleb had done. However, this time when I answered he sounded frantic and I could sense from his voice that something was terribly wrong. I could barely hear him because it was so noisy at the event, so I stepped only to hear John crying hysterically. He asked me to please hurry and get there because Caleb wasn't breathing. What? My heart sank to the pit of my stomach!

John told me to hold on because the police had just arrived, and he needed to answer the door. The timing couldn't have been any worse, the call dropped, and I was left with all kinds of negative thoughts scrambling through my mind. As I rushed back inside, my heart was racing, and I didn't know what to do! I asked everyone to please pray for Caleb because he had stopped breathing. John Called back and said that Caleb was breathing again and tried to explain what had happened. He said as Caleb was walking down the hall he heard a thud. He got up to check on him and found him lying on the floor. John attempted to pick him up and Caleb had a seizure, stopped breathing and was turning blue. He immediately started doing CPR and called 911. I could sense that John was having a breakdown and he just kept saying Cathy get here, please hurry get here. Cathy get here! I told John I didn't even know where his new house was. He was trying to explain to me, but I could barely understand him! Valeree from the Ranch said that she would drive me, so we jumped into her car and sped off in an attempt to try and find John's house. I was shaking so badly that I could barely type the address into map quest. John hung the phone up again only to call backto say that they had to intubate Caleb and that they were on the way to the hospital and for me to meet him there. We got to the hospital as fast as we could. Ij umped out of the car and rushed straight in to the front desk. I was so shaken that

I could hardly get my words out! They took me to the back immediately and all I saw was my son strapped to a gurney and doctor's rushing franticallyaround trying to figure out what was going on with him. John stood silently, and his face looked utterly terrified. He looked at me and began to cry! I asked him what happened, and he was trying so hard to compose himself, so he could explain. It was difficult for either of us to comprehend how we once again could be standing unexpectedly in the hospital with our precious little boy! How could all this be happening?

As I slowly approached Caleb's bed I could see that he was in bad shape. The grayish tinge had returned, and his fingers were bluer than usual. I knew that my lil man was in danger! I also noticed a cut on his mouth and asked John about it. He told me there were toy cars in the hall, so I immediately assumed that he was trying to ride one and slipped and fell knocking himself out. That was the only logical explanation that I could come up with for what possibly could have happened. The doctors were rushing around and running tests but were still unsure of exactly what had happened, so they were on the phone with Loma Linda. They immediately dispatched a helicopter to come get Caleb. I got on the phone and called Ashley and explained to her what was happening and that we were in Apple Valley at the hospital. I told her they were getting ready to send Caleb to Loma Linda! She began to cry, and I asked her if she would grab my bag and bring it to me. She knew there was always a bag beside my bed ready to go. She agreed and said that she would be right there. I told her how much I loved her, and we ended the call.

Ironically, my friend Brandy was one of the nurses taking care of Caleb! Thank God for her, she kept hugging me and reassuring me that Caleb was going to be ok. Ashley arrived, and I sent her over to the Ranch to pick up my car while we waited for transport. The test results were in and they were unable to find anything. The only thing that was certain was that his heart had been severely affected by the incident.

The team arrived, assessed Caleb and it was time for him to be flown to Loma Linda. We weren't allowed to go with him in the helicopter and would have to meet him there. We prayed over him and watched them put him in the helicopter. My heart was broken! The seriousness of  him having to be transported by helicopter put me in the state of mind of it being a life or death situation and that I may possibly never see my precious little Caleb again. As soon as he was finished being loaded into the helicopter, John and I jumped into my car and headed down to the hospital. John drove so we could get to our son quickly. We were yet again facing another long drive of not knowing what to expect once we got to the hospital. In the meantime, John just kept going over and over what had happened. He was distraught over the entire situation and was remorseful that it had even occurred. The only sensible thing that I could do was to keep saying the scripture I always quoted over Caleb. Youwill live and not die and declare the works of the Lord. We finally arrived at the hospital and thank God we were able to quickly find a parking spot and head right in. They informed us that Caleb was already in the CVICU. We headed up the elevator and once we got to the window the receptionist called back and they let us see him immediately.

We slowly walked into the room not knowing what to expect and to our astonishment there was Caleb with his eyes wide, looking back at us saying hi. We couldn't believe what we were seeing, he wasn't even intubated! John and I looked at each other and expressed our gratitude that our son was still alive! They were in the middle of doing an echo on him to see exactly what kind of damage had been done to his heart. Although he was extremely weak, he was still alive and yet fighting. I realized how much of a fighter that my little man was and just how great of a desire that he had to live. After the echo wascompleted, Dr. G who just happened to be on services that day, told us that Caleb's heart took a big hit and that he had suffered catastrophic heart failure. He followed up with the fact that Caleb was a very strong little boy and that they would do their best to figure out what exactly happened.We thanked him for his commitment to discover the underlying cause of such a horrific event.

They ran test after test and still had no idea as to what had happened. Because of severity of the incident, they were afraid Caleb's kidneys might not function properly.They were concerned that the heart failure could have adversely affected his ability to pee. We soon got our answer a few hours later when Caleb peed. Who would have ever thought that something we took for granted would ever be such a big deal! This victory proved to be agreat sign that Caleb was going to be ok!

Over the next few days Caleb's appetite increased and he was eating extremely well. He was regaining his strength back slowly but surely. He was in such a great mood that he even wanted to get up and sit in the chair. It took a lot out of him, but he was determined to make his big comeback. After all the tests had been conducted, they were still unsure of exactly what had happened. There was an enzyme test that would indicate his heart levels and if the numbers were decreasing they were satisfied. Each consecutive test indicated that his numbers were indeed decreasing. Long story short, Caleb was getting better!

Caleb was having a tough time keeping his oxygen levels where they normally should be. He needed a little help with keeping his oxygen saturation levels up. After all that he had been through it wasn't really a major concern for me because we had been on oxygen before. Shortly thereafter, we were able to wean him off and he was able to breath on his own once again. Things were happening so quickly that we viewed them as nothing short of a miracle. In our eyes, Caleb was the strongest boy ever! I just kept repeatedly praising God for all He was doing. They decided to do another echo to see if Caleb's heart was doing any better. Once the echo was completed, Dr. G came in and told us there was some improvement, but Caleb was still in severe heart failure. We had gone from catastrophic to severe but that was still an improvement! Caleb looked great and was in the best spirits. There was absolutely no way that I could be upset with the news from the echo!

Since Caleb was doing so well and had been cooped up in that room, we asked if it would be ok if we took him for a wagon ride. They agreed so it was off to the races for Caleb.

He was so excited, and he just loved riding in the wagon. Caleb was saying hi to everyone as we rolled by. The doctors and nurses were also elated to see him out and about. He was still eating great and getting better by the day. John's girlfriend had also been at the hospital on many occasions to offer her support. 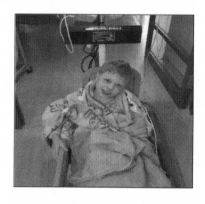 It was very hard for me but because of the circumstances I had to set my feelings aside and do what was best for Caleb. That day we ended up having a much-needed talk and she apologized for everything that had taken place in the past. She went on to explain that she regretted being selfish and that she was truly sorry. She even went as far as to take ownership for what she had done wrong and that she was aware that it was something she would have to live with for the rest of her life. I thanked her as well as expressed the pain that it had caused me. For the longest I had wrestled in my mind with how anyone could have done this to another person, especially knowing they were married and caring for a very ill child. The sad part is that just the year prior, we had all went to an amusement park together. She went with one of John's friend's. As the conversation progressed I explained that it was extremely difficult to forgive her because not only did she take my husband, she also took my son's father. By the expression on her face, I knew that those words had a deep impact on her. I further elaborated that John spent more time with her than with his own son. She initially didn't want to accept that but as she pondered on it she seemed to see it from my perspective. We decided to place the entire ordeal to the side and focus on Caleb because that was what was most important. We couldn't turn back the hands of time and undo anything, so from here on out Caleb would be top priority. We would all be #teamcaleb!

Caleb was getting stronger and stronger. The doctors were impressed with his progress, so they decided to allow him to go for a walk. A walk! Can you believe it? That was so exciting! We got him ready and set out on our journey. There was an entire team of people cheering Caleb on. We knew we were well on our way to recovery. John and I had talked to the doctor's and just knew we would be on our way home soon. Caleb was on top of the world, flexing his muscles for the nurses and back to his charming self. He was such a charmer, and everyone loved him so much.

Caleb's tests were all coming back great and even the enzyme test was showing improvement. It looked like we would begetting discharged in no time. Dr. K came into check on Caleb and had a talk with us. He explained that all the doctors had talked and that they were convinced that Caleb had experienced a sudden death event. Dr. K explained that it wasn't uncommon for someone such as Caleb. He went on to tell us that since Stanford was ready to proceed with the transplant, that instead of us going home they were already getting things in motion to transport him there. What? We thought we were on our way home and now this! It was definitely not the newswe thought we were going to receive. My heart sank, and I didn't know what to think.We weren't prepared for this. In the past we had plenty of time to prepare but not this time.W eweren't ready. The plan was already in motion and like it or not we were going to Stanford.

John and I went back and forth on who would fly with Caleb. John decided it would be best for him to go because I had things to take care of. We also knew that if we were going to transplant that I would be there for a long time and needed to get my car. John and I were overwhelmed with emotions and it was too much for either one of us. We knew all that went into a transplant and we were both extremely apprehensive. We called everyone to tell them the change of plans. They all came to the hospital that eveningto spend time with Caleb before his trip. Caleb was enthused to see everyone, and it brought comfort to see him happy.

Today Caleb would be heading to Stanford. The crew came and got him ready for the flight. John was stressed out but we both knew that this was the best plan for Caleb and as much as we didn't want it to happen, we had to trust the doctor's. I walked with Caleb and John to the ambulance that would transport them to the airfield where the plane awaited. We prayed over Caleb and away they went. I was a mess and couldn't stop crying. It was a nightmare. I had to get home and get things in order, so I could head up to Stanford. It was so upsetting, and everyone agreed I shouldn't drive there alone. Derane agreed to ride with me and I was grateful for his kindness. Deep down I knew that I was in no shape to drive that far alone. While I was at home getting things together I just lost it. The burden had simply become too much to handle. I was broken and hurting so badly for my son. I had no idea what Caleb's life would be like from here on out. A flurry of thoughts filled my mind to include good as well as bad. However, I must admit that the vast majority were bad. Whatever the outcome may be, we had no choice but to accept it and deal with it.

I finally received a call from John letting me know that they had arrived safely. John told me that he was glad he decided to go with Caleb because it was a small plane and that he even had a hard time with the flight. I tried to choke back the tears as I thanked him for sacrificing that for us. He told me once they had Caleb settled in his room they started running their own tests trying to figure out what had happened. Just as before all of their tests came back with the same results. We were still unclear as to exactly what had happened. In spite of the uncertainty, we were still moving forward to determine if Caleb was eligible for a new heart. In my desperation I prayed that we would get the answers we were seeking and that soon we would be placing Caleb on the transplant list.

I had gotten everything in order, was all packed and ready for the trip. I went to get gas before Derane and I headed to Stanford. My phone rang, and it was John. He was upset and told me don't get upset but Caleb just did it again. John said Caleb was using the bathroom and the next thing he knew, Caleb's eyes rolled back, and he went out. John said he yelled for the nurse and quickly placed Caleb on the bed. He said the doctor's ran in and started performing CPR. Caleb was still alive, but the doctors were working hard to get him back. I told him that maybe Caleb is tired of fighting. He could possibly be trying to let us know that he is ready to go! It was by far the hardest thing I ever thought I would have to say but I didn't want to be selfish. If Caleb was ready we would have to let him go! John yelled at met hat he couldn't let his son go! He loudly exclaimed that Caleb was having another episode and hung up on me. I was horrified! I assumed that Caleb was dying and on his way to Heaven. At that moment I had peace unlike anything I had ever experienced before came over me. I saw Andre and we just sat there. He asked if I was ok and I said I don't know but I'm pretty sure

Caleb has died. H eheld me and kept telling me that he was sorry! Andre kept telling me everything would be ok. I didn't know what to do or where to go. I was at a loss for words.

I called Ashley and told her what John had said and that Caleb was gone. I also called my friend Ken and explained the terrible turn of events to him. He asked where I was and said that he would be right over. Both of my friends were so supportive! They were trying to comfort me asking if I was ok, but they were totally unaware of the amazing sense of peace that I was experiencing. About 45 minutes later Ashley called me and told me that Caleb hadn't died! He was still here and doing just fine! Wow!

I switched gears and met up with Derane and we headed up to Stanford. On the way there, I spoke with John several times. He told me that Dr.H decided to insert a pacemaker into Caleb so that if his heart did that again the pacemaker would shock his heart and put it back on rhythm. John said we had to be very careful about stimulating him because they were all nervous that it could possibly cause him to relapse again. After what seemed like the longest drive ever, Derane and I finally made it. We rushed up to see Caleb and he was bubbling with joy to see us. I hugged him tightly and there aren't words that can describe how it felt to hold him in my arms once again.

We all were to mindful not to excite him, so we carried about as calmly as we possibly could. John looked drained, so I told him to go and get some rest and that I would take over. He explained that he was having a hard time closing his eyes because all he could see was Caleb having the incidents, especially the one at his house .He then went on to tell me that he had never seen Caleb that blue and that he knew he was dying right before his eyes. I began to cry and told him that I was sorry. I could see in his eyes that the memories haunted him terribly. In an effort to encourage him, I thanked him for saving our son's life. I also took the opportunity to remind him that although we were going through a difficult time, I still needed him to be strong for Caleb and me. There was no way I could doi t all by myself and we needed him. Although it was a struggle for me to admit it, I knew that I needed John there more than ever. We had a long road ahead of us, so I let John get some rest and I went back in the room with Caleb. I snuggled up with Caleb and it felt amazing to be next to my baby.

We were up bright and early. It was time for Caleb to have his pacemaker inserted. We walked with him as we always did, said our prayer and held him as they gassed him off to sleep. Dr. H of course, went over the negative and positive aspects of the placement. He expressed his concerns because of Caleb's heart function and anesthesia. He concluded by stating that Caleb was one of the strongest boys he had ever known, and he just knew that he would do great. We went to our usual stop and waited. John's girlfriend, his brother and his brother's wife came for support. I was very glad because John definitely needed the support of family after all that had happened.

Dr. H came out after a very short time. I was startled because Caleb's procedures never go that fast. The closer he got the further I stepped back. We had fought so hard to get to this point and I was praying and hoping that it wouldn't be the end of our journey. Dr. H smiled and said, "Where are you going." All the while trembling I said, "I don't know I'm just scared." He responded with, "Get over here Caleb did great!" Wow! What a relief! He informed us that it was actually easier than he thought it would be. He opened Caleb up from the bottom and his heart popped right out and he was able to place the pacemaker and the wires effortlessly. He even said his heart looked very good and that his squeeze looked good in spite of all the incidents. That was all we needed to hear. It was music to our ears when he said if Caleb does well we should be able to get out of there within a few days. From there it would be back to the Ronald McDonald house, because of all that Caleb had been through they decided to leave him on the vent, so he could rest and tomorrow they would take him off. He really needed to get some rest in order to hasten the recovery process. We received the call from the Ronald McDonald house, so we went over to check in. It was crazy to imagine us all checking into the house together, but we were now officially #teamcaleb.

Caleb was gradually weaning off of the vent and ready to be extubated. The doctors came in once Caleb was awake and removed the tube. Caleb did great! Praise God he was breathing on his own but his lungs were pretty junky so that meant lots of chest PT. We had to get him better because they had already scheduled his transplant heart cath for the 26th. Although he didn't have much of an appetite, with some coaxing he was soon wanting to take bites. He was back to eating and that was amazing.

The next few days were pretty good as well. Caleb's lungs were getting better, and he was progressively gaining his strength back. The doctors were concerned with the amount of weight that he had lost so they left the NG tube in and they decided to do continuous feeds to help him gain it back. We definitely needed to get weight on him before the transplant took 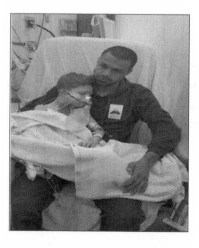 place. Caleb was determined to move forward and decided to get up and walk around. It tired him out but how amazing it was to witness his perseverance. God is so good.

The day arrived for the transplant heart cath. They needed to go in and look at everything especially Caleb's lung pressures. The pressures would determine if his little body could handle a new full heart. Again, like always we went down with Caleb, said a prayer and held him until he was fast asleep. We all headed to the waiting area to sit and wait. This was a monumental moment because it was the last test to determineif Caleb would qualify for a new whole heart. It took a few hours, but the doctor came out and told us that Caleb did great. We discussed the numbers and he told usvwhat was observed. Hevexplained thatvnot only was Caleb's Heart function better, but that his squeeze was also much better then when he had first arrived. He went on to inform us that the pressures in his lungs were a bit higher than they normally liked but not so much that he couldn't receive a new heart. He made a note that it was totally up to the transplant doctors now. I asked if Caleb would be going back on the vent and he let us know that they had already taken the vent out but were going to leave him on oxygen to assist his lungs. Caleb would be back in his room shortly and we couldn't wait! About thirty minutes later he came rolling in. He was a little groggy, but he was awake. We let him relax for the rest of the day. That evening Caleb was asking for water which was a very good sign. They let him drink a little here and there throughout the night.

It was a new day and Caleb was in an excellent mood. It was determined that he could eat so we ordered him breakfast and to our surprise he ate it all. Afterwards, Caleb seemed to have some energy so the doctor's thought it be good for him to get up and walk being that walking is especially good for the lungs. As we set out, we could tell that his body was sore and still weak from the pacemaker placement. He was a little slow but at least he was up and moving about. It may seem insignificant to others but to us it was classified as a miracle. The doctors even ordered that Caleb be weaned from IV meds to oral. If that wasn't amazing enough, I received a call from our local paper saying that they wanted to do a story to let our community know how Caleb was doing. The story went out later that night online and was printed the next day. Just to think that my son's life was so impacting that it wouldnow be broadcasted for others to see. People loved my sweet boy so much and were very concerned about him. #team-caleb was off to a strong start.

The next few days were spent focusing on Caleb and working on getting him stronger. He was eating and playing more and even able to be removed from oxygen. Caleb was such a strong lil fella. The transplant doctors had made their determination if Caleb was able to be listed and receive his new heart. They had set up a meeting with all the doctors to go over their decision. John and I had been talking. We were so undecided after all that Caleb had been through if we even wanted to put Caleb through a heart transplant. We thought that maybe we should just let whatever days Caleb had left be the best they could possibly be and maybe we should just leave our baby alone.

It was time for our meeting and we both were very nervous knowing that the meeting would determine what our next step would be. We sat and waited for everyone to show up. Once everyone was presentt hey started going over all the information the tests had shown them. The moment came when they would render their decision. Time seemed to stand still as the transplant doctor said we all have come to the conclusion that at this time Caleb is NOT an ideal candidate for a heart transplant. We both were floored to hear those words. I started crying uncontrollably. The doctor went on to explain that Caleb's body wasn't strong enough to receive a new heart. Although it was a no for now, we were given the opportunity to get him stronger and come back at a later date to see if he was ready. John and I thanked them for making the difficult decision for us. We explained that before the meeting we were talking and were much undecided if we even wanted to put Caleb through that. We were so grateful that they had made the choice for us so that we didn't have to. They said they would get Caleb started on palliative care and make sure he was comfortable in the days to come. As heartbroken as we were at least we had the answer. They immediately proceeded to get the discharge papers ready for us to leave that day. The sooner Caleb got home to rest would be the better for him. We checked Caleb out of the hospital and stayed at the Ronald McDonald house that night. We decided we would rest and meditate on everything that had recently taken place. The next day we would head home and figure out what the game plan was for our next move concerning Caleb.

We packed up the car and were headed off back to Barstow. It was a long trip and Caleb was still pretty weak, but we were just glad to be heading home. I wished the outcome was different but there wasn't anything we could do except what the doctors had suggested and check back at a later date. Until then we plannedto make the best of the time we had. We finally made it home and after dropping her off to get their car, John drove with me and Caleb to my house. After we were situated, John left, and Caleb and I snuggled in for the night. There were so many calls to want and come see Caleb. I agreed but I also told them that Caleb needed his rest. It was a great feelingto be in the comforts of my own home. Now I could focus solely on getting Caleb well and putting some weight back on him.

The calls started coming in from Loma Linda to set up appointments to get Caleb started on palliative care. That was a little hard to take because the reality was that this program was just the step prior to hospice. I wanted Caleb to have everything he needed so I obliged and began to set up the appointments. On a side note, I noticedthatCaleb was starting to get a cough and runny nose. I thought not again I just got him home and better.

I received a call from Robin Lard telling me that she wanted to include Caleb in her Heart for a Hero program. We both started to cry as I said yes, we would be honored. Robin said because Caleb was a very special boy that she wanted to do something very special for him. She had reached out to different people and theyall made valentine cards for Caleb. Robin explained how Caleb had touched her and gave so many courage through his bravery that they all wanted to give their hearts for Valentine's Day to Caleb. She said he was their hero!

We went for Caleb's follow-up appointment with Dr. B at Loma Linda. The doctor waspleasedwith the way Caleb's incision looked and removed his stitches. We were so thankful to be finally moving in the right direction. Having the stitches removed meant that his incision was healed. We were extremely thankful!

Caleb wasn't feeling well and was running a fever. I noticed Caleb's incision didn't look too good either, so I called Jennifer at Loma Linda and she said bring him in right away. We loaded Caleb into the car and headed there. In my mind I thought it would be something simple not realizing how dangerous it actually was. They kept us and explained that if the infection spread to his pace-maker they would have to remove it and start the processall over again. I definitely wasn't prepared for that. They prepared his room and explained that he would have to go in for surgery the next day to clean out his wound. They also explained the incision would have to stay open and heal from the inside out. John and I were a little taken back by this, so I got on the phone and called Ashley. I asked her once again if she could grab my bag and said that we would be staying. My poor son was once again at place of uncertainty.

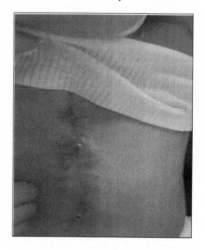

Time for Caleb to go in and get his incision cleaned out. Prayers went up as we held Caleb until he was under the anesthesia. We went down and waited for him. The procedure was quick and the next thing we knew Caleb was back in his room and we could go see him. He was awake watching TV like nothing had happened. He was also telling me to look while pointing to his chest. I got in the bed and snuggled with him. My son was so strong and how much I loved that little boy. I knew we weren't out of the woods yet, but I was truly thankful to still have him here with us. They started Caleb on high powered antibiotics to make sure the infection was alleviated and didn't spread to the pacemaker. They ran tests and thank God they all came back negative. The infection at this point was only in his incision. A wound vac was utilized on him to help keep his wound dry and also keep his little fingers out. The dressing had to be changed every other day. On top of that, Caleb didn't like it on his chest and he kept telling me ow,ow, ow. I felt so bad for him. He now had to deal with an NG tube, Pic line, and a wound vac. My poor baby.

Days passed, and Caleb got diarrhea from all of the antibiotics. We had to keep a diaper on him because he wasn't able to make it to the bathroom. His poor little heinie was so red and had a serious rash. They prescribed medicine, but nothing seemed to work.The doctor's asked if John and I felt comfortable taking Caleb home. They believed that he had the possibility of doing much better at home. We talked it over and decided we would take him home. They ordered all of his meds which totaled about 15 and also nurses to come every other day to the house to change his dressings. They trained us on how to administer the meds. We had never done a pic-line before and honestlyt hat pic-line scared me to death. It went straight into his bloodstream. We had to be very careful because that was a major source of opportunity for infection among other things. I wasn't sure if I could handle that. But I knew in my heart that Caleb would do better at home. John and I both took turns changing the line and we were surprisingly confident in being ready to take Caleb home.

We got Caleb home and seemed happy to be there. We were Team Caleb and collectively decided we would all stay at my house. I know that it sounds outlandish, but Caleb needed John and me both if he was going to get better. Like I said that pic-line scared me to death and John wasn't bothered by it at all. Caleb wasn't sleeping well so John and I took shifts so that we could get some rest. Caleb was very sick, and we just wanted the best for him.

We had an appointment with Dr. B to check Caleb's incision. Dr. B evaluated Caleb and decided that he no longer needed the wound vac. Praise God! One thing down now 3 more to go. We needed to finish the antibiotics, get the pic-line out and also try getting the NG tube out. John and I decided it was best to put in the feeding tube that would go straight into Caleb's belly. We still had hopes of getting him stronger and maybe one day qualifying for a heart, but for now it was one step at a time. We got the wound vac off and that was a relief. Caleb still had very itchy skin, so we decided to keep the incision covered. We definitely didn't want it to get infected again.

We still were making frequent visits to Loma Linda because Dr. B wanted to keep a close eye on Caleb. Dr. B still wasn't convinced that the infection hadn't spread to his pacemaker. I was praying that it hadn't. We were on the countdown till the antibiotics were going to be finished and we couldn't wait to get the pic-line out of Caleb's arm. We kept school going and tried to keep life as normal as possible. It was so sad that Caleb was getting to the point where he didn't even want to get out of bed. I tried really hard to keep his spirits up and even consistently took him outside to get sun hoping it would help him feel better. While Caleb was in the hospital, his classroom made him a huge get-well card and all the student's signed it. His teacher asked if she could stop by to see Caleb and bring the card. I told her that would be great, and it cheered Caleb up to see her. It was nice to see my boy smiling again.

Caleb received some very special mail. Because of Robin doing the Heart for a Hero, Vanessa reached out to Robin and asked if it would be ok if she sent Caleb some Golden Books with signed autographs. Caleb was so excited, he absolutely loved books. I read them to him as he rested in the bed. I was happy to see all the people who loved him and reaching out hoping to make him feel better.#teamcalebrocks.

Caleb was still pretty blue and not feeling well. I could hear the congestion in his lungs. I was extremely concerned. He seemed depressed, so I called Camille and she suggested taking him to the dollar store and letting him pick out whatever he wanted. It was a great idea and John and I did just that. I called Ashley, Marianne, and Erica and told them what we had planned. I also told them after we were done we were going to the park. Caleb lit up as he picked out random items. I didn't care about the cost because more importantly he was laughing and smiling!

They all eventually met up with us at the store and by the end of the spree Caleb had picked out thirty-five dollars' worth of stuff. Bubbles, a kite, bat and ball were among the things he chose. After we paid it was off to the park for some fun in the sun. We blew bubbles, flew kites, and Caleb was even  hitting the ball with the bat. He seemed to become fatigued fairly quickly, but he was still havinga great time. My mom even walked up to the park to hang out with us. It made everyone's day just seeingCaleb enjoying himself. I dreaded the day coming to an end and Caleb having to return home. We loved watching him enjoy himself.

I was progressively becoming more discouraged because I had been doing everything within my ability to help Caleb get better, but nothing seemed to be working. I was crying out to the

Lord asking Him to give me direction as He had done before in the past. I just couldn't seem to get Caleb's diarrhea to clear up. His appetite wasn't getting any better either. I was so thankful for his NG tube because without it I don't know how Iwould have gotten him to eat! I honestly felt like I was failing him. I was overwhelmed, and the struggle was getting harder and harder. Caleb wasn't doing well at all and he had so many different things going on. To top it off, he was still having trouble breathing. I was so worried I decided to take him to the Barstow ER. The doctor ran tests and did an x-ray. After all the test results were in he discovered thatCaleb had thrush, a yeast infection, and something that looked like walking pneumonia. The doctor wrote a prescription and we went home. At least we had some answers and along with the new medications maybe I would be able to get him well.

Caleb and I were both sick but thankfully Caleb was feeling a little better. I had caught what Caleb had and I was feeling horrible. I knew if I felt that bad thenCaleb must have felt ten times worse. John came to get Caleb for his visit and Caleb was excited to see him. I was so worried about Caleb that I kept calling and checking on him. I was hoping that going to his dad's house might cheer him up but soon discovered that it didn't help either. No matter what we did Caleb still wasn't doing well. He only seemed to be getting worse.

I made a call to Jennifer at Loma Linda. She wanted Caleb to come in so that they could put eyes on him. They still weren't convinced the infection hadn't spread to his pacemaker. I was sick, so John had to take him in. Once they were there they ran additional tests. They decided they were going to keep Caleb and stop feeding him for a bit to give his gut a rest. I was so saddened that I wasn't able to be with Caleb. They did an echo and Dr. G said his heart function was great and was the best he had seen in a long time. Although that was hopeful news, all of the rest didn't seem to coincide.

John and I weren't happy with one another, and it was becoming more challenging to talk to him. He was very short on words and outright mean to me. I knew that he was stressed out and that he was accustomed to having me there to help. He sent me a picture of Caleb and his heinie and the look on Caleb's face said it all. Because they decided to stop feeding him, the diarrhea became acidic and it literally burned away the top layer of Caleb's bottom. Every time he'd go to the bathroom it would burn him and his skin became raw skin. I told John that we needed to have a tube inserted into his colon, so the fecal matter wouldn't have to make contact with his skin. It was such a painful ordeal that they started giving him morphine to help ease the pain.

John called me to clarify that Caleb did not have walking pneumonia, he instead had influenza B. John's voice was shaky and the fact that I wasn't there was extremely hard on both of us. I felt horrible. Never in Caleb's whole life had I not been able to be there. I felt so helpless and as much as John and I fought I knew he was depending on me for such times. I was literally heartbroken. I felt so bad for John that he had to handle it all on his own. All the while my poor baby was suffering and in so much pain.

Caleb was still struggling with the stool issue and the tube had not yet been implemented. I repeatedly calledthe hospital to try and figure out what was going on. John was beyond stressed out and definitely taking his frustrations out on me. I knew he was having a difficult time, but the misguided frustrations were simply unacceptable. I stopped communicating with him all together and decided to receive updates from the nurse. Caleb was in the worst pain of his life and his lungs continued to get worse. I felt helpless and deep inside wished that there was some way that I could be there for him.

I desperately wanted Caleb to feel better, soI came up with the idea of hiring someone to dress up like Elsa from Frozen to go and hold Caleb's hand because I couldn't be there. He absolutely loved the movie Frozen and I figured it would at least brighten his day a little. I made a ton of phone calls but wasn't able to find one person to do it. It was so disheartening that I wasn't able to come through for my baby.

My phone rang, and it was John. The trembling in his voice once again sounded oh so familiar. My heart started racing as he followed with I needed to get there ASAP. I initially thought that the call would simply be to update me, but it was far from that. To lessen my fears, I asked him if it was bad and he responded with if it wasn't he wouldn't be calling me! He said, "Hurry!" I hung up the phone trembling. God please help me! I gathered my things and headed to Loma Linda. Jennifer and Irene also called me on the way down asking me if I was ok, so I knew it wasn't good.

I couldn't get there fast enough. I finally arrived and called John while on my way up to the room. He met me in the hall and informed me that Caleb was receiving Morphine every two hours. I hurried in to see Caleb only to find him resting. My poor baby's lips were bluer than I had ever seen before. The doctors were scrambling around, and I knew what that meant. They told me that they had just ran a test and that Caleb wasn't oxygenating well at all. They were going to have to intubate him. Caleb looked like he was literally teetering on the edge of life. After intubation I could feel him coming back to us and he began to rest comfortably.

My nerves were shot and began to manifest through panic attacks. I knew things had to be taking a toll on John as well. They worked through the night trying to stabilize Caleb. One of the blood test results was through the roof which meant that Caleb could start to bleed to death at any moment. They immediately administered medication to thicken his blood. John and I were exhausted and went to lay down in our cars to try and get some rest. Unfortunately, I couldn'tsleep and continued to have anxiety attacks.

Unable to sleep, I decided to check on Caleb and that's when they asked if they could put in a pic line. The upside is that they wouldn't have to keep sticking Caleb. I agreed that was best and after many unsuccessful attempts they were finally able to get one in. It took over an hour. I went to peek in on Caleb with the intentions of requesting that they stop if the pic line wasn't installed by then. While looking through the window of his room the doctor gave me the thumbs up. The happiness was short lived when they used it once and it blew.

The doctors needed access, so they asked if it would be ok to puti n an a trial line. I said whatever is best but if they ran into trouble I didn't want them sticking Caleb over and over. He had been through enough already, so I was thankful when the line went in fairly quickly. Once that was completed I assumed that Caleb could rest but that wasn't the case. As soon as they got everything cleaned up, Caleb coded and they all rushed back in trying to bring him back. There was so much going on simultane-ously. Someone was doing chest compressions, one doctor was shouting for medications to be administered, machines were going off and one of the nurses was bagging Caleb trying to get his numbers to come back up. I stood there frozen, watching them work diligently to bring Caleb back. Thankfully their efforts were successful.

I called John and told him what had just happened, and he was there in a matter of minutes. We both were such a mess. We got on the phone and started calling everyonewe could possibly think of to hurry there. It was almost 4am and John and I both felt that Caleb was preparing to transition into eternity. We encouraged everyone to come and say their final goodbyes to Caleb. It was probably the hardest news ever to deliver. It was a hard pill to swallow that Caleb more than likely wasn't going to recover this time.We were certain that it would be the last stop for our precious Caleb. After the phone calls were done, John and I had a serious talk. We knew that there would come a day when we would have to set boundariesas to what we would allow to be done to Caleb. If the requests were outside of those boundaries, then we knew that it was time to let Caleb go. We agreed to no more shocking him and if he coded again no more chest compressions. As hard as it was, we had drawn our line. We held on to one another and cried. We knew we were losing our son.

Everyone started to show up for support and to say their final goodbyes. Caleb's numbers were horrible, and his oxygen stats were 32. His little hands were tightening up and it was almost as if he were having seizures. He was intubated but yet still struggling to take breaths. There was nothing we could do but simply stand there watching and waiting for him to die. I felt so helpless. I cried out to the nurse to help my baby boy. I told her I didn't want him to feel any pain. She ran out and got some medication. They decided to give him some Ativan to take the edge off. As soon as she gave it to him his little fingers relaxed, and he looked much better.

I looked up and everyone was gathering in the room. Ashley, Samantha, Erica, Johanna, Cindi, Lisa, Melissa, Robin, Ms. Muir, John'sfamily, and even some of her family came. Caleb was struggling to even exist. He was purple and taking shallow sips of air. The doctors came in 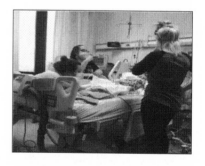 and said we were probably going to have to make some decisions on how we were going to let our son go. I collapsed over Caleb and beganto wail unlike any of the previous times. I cried out to God saying that I had done everything He asked me to do for Caleb! Please Lord don't make me do this. You are the giver and taker of life please Lord! Please don't make me choose this for my son. I knew thatCaleb was giving his last, final effort before transitioning and was trying to draw from strength that he discovered was no longer there. I whispered in his ear thatI loved him so much, but it was time for him to go. I told him that he didn't belong here anymore. I looked to John and I told him that he had to tell him it was ok to leave because if not he would stay! John was reluctant at first but then whispered in his ear telling him how much he loved him! He said it's ok son, you can go now!! We both lost it and held onto Caleb for dear life.

The doctor's wanted to speak with John and I in another room so that we could make the decisions but before they met with us Dr. AL asked if it would be ok if she gave Caleb some blood, changed his vent settings and start him on nitric gas. She knew what our line was and although John and I both were very upset we agreed to give it a shot. I was crying so hard that I couldn't even see through the tears. I told Dr. AL. I couldn't do it and she said that Caleb was in God's hands. She also told me that I could do it or else He would have never given him to me. Dr. AL. wanted to give it a try now that the ball was in Caleb's court. If he wanted to live he would and if he was ready to leave he would do just that.

They made the changes and drew a blood gas before we went to talk to the team about what we were going to do. John and I went into the small waiting room, the one we had been in so many times before but today it seemed even smaller. We waited for the doctor's and the social worker to come in. Shortly after entering and having a seat, one of the doctors saidthat the blood gas indicated that Caleb was doing much better and that he just might actually pull through. I couldn't believe my ears, was he serious? I knew Caleb had done this so many times in the past. He would walk right up to the edge and then do a complete turn-around. Was he doing it again? Was Caleb about to wow us all by pulling through this one too?

The doctor's and social worker expressed that we should still have the talk just in case Caleb took a turn for the worse, they would already know what our desires were. They gave us the options and the first one was to remove the breathing tube. I stopped him in his tracks by saying that I would never do that. I could never watch my son gasping for his last breath. After thatI didn't care to hear any more options. I interjected that if I had to choose a way, I would just slowly turn down his support medications and allow him to transition on his own. John was having such a difficult time with the conversation all together, he just cried silently. I told everyone in the room that I was at peace with it and I was tired of torturing my son. I felt that John wasn't ready so out of respect for him I was willing to do anything up to the point where we drew our line.

We went back into the room and sure enough Caleb was indeed doing better. His stats were back up to where they normally were, and he was actually looking much better. The child life specialist came in and we all ended up doing hand prints with Caleb. Everyone was in and out all day laughing and loving on Caleb. The day literally went from a tragedy to a triumph. I couldn't believe that Caleb had once again eluded death and decided to stay. My cousins Melissa and Jayson had come to support us. We hadn't talked in years because of all the things that had happened over time. I began to ponder how it often takes a tragedy to bring people together.

To celebrate we all decided to go out to dinner. I was trying to enjoy my time with everyone, but my heart was at the hospital with Caleb. After dinner I went back to the hospital to hang outwith Caleb. He again was only allowed to have 2 visitors at a time and was back on the routinely scheduled visits. We were thankful that Camille had rented us a room for two day sright before she left because we didn't have anywhere else to stay. The Ronald McDonald house was full once again, so it really meant a lot for her to do that for us.

Everyone was gathered in the lobby, so I decided to utilize the opportunity to bring awareness to being there for one another. I told them that it was unfortunate that many of us only came together when a tragedy occurred. I expressed the fact that I was literally exhausted from the journey of caring for Caleb. I would desperately need everyone's help with Caleb once we got home and I wouldn't be able to do it without them. I genuinely posed the question of could we be the #teamcaleb that he truly needed us to be. I was in tears when one by one they came up and hugged me and promised that they would be there more from now on. Many of John's family members apologized for not being there and offered heartfelt words of encouragement.

Later on, John and I talked again, and he suggested that I get some rest and that he would stay with Caleb that night. Although I appeared to still be pressing forward, on the inside I was at the point of breaking down. I desperately needed rest. As I was preparing to leave, Ryan came in and wanted to pray for Caleb. It was ironic that as we talked he said that Caleb was preaching to us all from his hospital bed and that he was doing so without even saying one word. That was true! He was so right. We simply stood there in amazement.

After praying for Caleb, I kissed and hugged him and told him how much that he meant to me.I was extremely tired, so I went back to the room. I took a shower and tried to relax but I just couldn't. My mind was still on Caleb, so I called the hospital a few times to talk with the nurse. She reassured me that my little man was doing well and that he was on his best behavior. She had given him a bath and he was doing just fine. She also promised that ifanything changed she would call me ASAP. I felt better and tried to get some rest.

I was up early and called to talk to the nurse before shift change to see how Caleb had done throughout the night. She said that he had did great and that all of his labs looked amazing! Wow! What a relief. We headed out andcouldn't wait to get to Caleb's room. All I wanted was to love on him. Ashley and I went in and to our surprise he looked great. His numbers were all stable and he was looking like his old self. What a difference a day could make. Family and friends started arriving to include John's mom and brother DJ from Vegas. They all took turns going up and spending time with him. It was great to see them doing what they said they would do. While groups of 2 visited Caleb, the rest of us sat in the lobby and enjoyed snacks that Johns sister Nikki had brought. My granddaughter Hannah was tired, so the girls went back to the room to take a nap. I could see that it was taking a toll on us all.

Once they left, I decided to go see Caleb. I hadn't been in the room for quite some time due to everyone else having a turn. Nikki wanted to go with me, so we made our way on up. We greeted him before sitting down and could feel a calmness in the room. Caleb's numbers offered a great sense of hope. We watched as the respiratory therapist administered treatment to get his lungs up to par. As he coughed he cringed and we could tell that it was causing him a great deal of pain. His nurse ironically, was the same one that had cared for him after he was born. I loved her so much and was so glad to see her. During the treatment Caleb's heart rate was all over the place. I made mention of it to her but she didn't seem too worried about it. She said he was probably just a little upset and that he would eventually calm down. Although she remained calm the entire time, I on the other hand was a nervous wreck. I had asked a thousand questions before she said,"Don't worry Cathyleen you know how Caleb does." We both started to laugh.

The nurse was in the process of changing his epinephrine. She disconnected it andimmediately hooked the other one up. In just thatshort period there was a drastic turn of events. His numbers started to fall, and his blood pressure got very low. The nurse said she was afraid it would happen. I immediately stood up ands tarted rubbing on Caleb because I had seen this before! WhenCaleb was under deep sedation his pressures would get soft.

She sped up the pace drastically trying to get Caleb's numbers up. I began to tell him that it's mama and that I needed him to wake up a little and to get his numbers back up. I knew that he heard me because although he was facing the total opposite direction, he turned to where I was. He was struggling to open his eyes but couldn't because he was so sedated. He was trying his best to look at me. He started rubbing his face on the pillow as if he were doing it to my cheek. It felt like he was trying to tell me I love you mama. It was at that moment that his head slumped, and all of his numbers plummeted. The nurse responded by hitting the code button. I ran out of the room to find John. I hit the elevator buttons and the doors opened immediately. My heart was racing while descending to the lobby. The doors opened, and I ran into the lobby. John was standing up and saw me. He rushed over, and I yelled,"It's happening again."John cursed and jumped into the elevator. I felt light headed and had to sit down. John's girlfriend and I were sitting there, and her phone rang. She answered and cried out no! She said it was concerning Caleb and was I going back up. I told her no because I was already aware of what was taking place. I couldn't bear to watch it! She left and went up to the room. I just sat there knowing that he was dying. Suddenly, I had a feeling of peace come over me that no words can describe. God was surrounding me with His love and I knew my son was free and in the arms of the Lord.

My phone rang, and they asked me to come back up. As soon as the doors opened the doctor was standing there waiting for me. He looked at me and said that Caleb was gone. I told them I already knew. They asked me if I was ok and I told them that strangely, somehow, I was, I was glad my baby was finally free. I asked them if they could please clean him up and remove everything. I knew everyone would want to see him. Dr.G hugged me and told me he was sorry. He said, "Just wait here while I go back in and shut off his pacemaker." I made sure to thank him for all he had done for Caleb! The elevator doors opened again, and

John's brother exited with a distraught look on his face. He was in tears and he hugged me while expressing how sorry he was. Soon after the girls came frantically running out asking how he was doing. I had no choice but to tell them that he was no longer with us. Erica collapsed to the floor and started crying uncontrollably. It felt as if things were moving in slow motion as the girls held on to one another weeping. I can't describe what it felt like at that moment. I was overwhelmed with emotion as I embraced the reality that my son had just passed from this life into the next. I hurt so badly but at the same time I was relieved that Caleb could now soar with his wings in a place of no more pain and limitations. My baby had finished his race and had crossed the finish line. No more surgeries, no more sticks, no more tests, my son was finally whole and in the arms of our Heavenly Father. Oh, how I wished I could have seen the expression on his face as he first laid eyes on his new permanent residence of eternity!

Jennifer stayed with me to ensure I was ok. She asked me if I wanted to go see Caleb and I told her I wasn't sure if I could. She was aware that he would be cremated so she gently reminded me that this would be the last time I would be able to see him. I nodded yes and slowly followed after her. She used her badge to open the doors and all the nurses were standing there crying. They took turns hugging me and offering their condolences. I thanked them and expressed how grateful I was for everything they had done. I also noted that because they trained me so well, I was able to care for Caleb at home properly and it was because of them that he was able to stay with us as long as he did. They cared for him as if he were their very own child.

Dr. AL came out of Caleb's room and gave me the biggest hug. Tears were streaming from her eyes as she said Caleb is now in the safest place. I thanked her for all of her efforts towards Caleb. Afterwards, I slowly made my way down to his room. I positioned myself so that my back was turned to the opening of the door. I was trying to find the strength to turn around and look at my baby. I finally mustered up the courage to peek into the room. At a glance I could see Caleb lying there with John. Trembling with fear, Jennifer took my hand and we entered the room. I wasn't willing to accept what my eyes were seeing. My son's body was lying there lifeless. John seemed to be in a daze as he softly rubbed Caleb's chest sobbing. I bent down and hugged Caleb. He smelled like he had just taken a bath. I inhaled a deep breath of his Johnson and Johnson's baby lotion. That was enough for me, I couldn't take it. My heart had shattered into a thousand pieces. I kissed him and told him how thankful I was for the privilege of being his mama. I told him how much I loved him! I couldn't handle seeing my baby like that! John requested to watch Yo Gabba Gabba one more time with Caleb. The nurse turned it on and by the time the Goodbye song played I was finished, I had to get out of there! I smelled my baby's stinky little toes one last time and I departed. I couldn't do it anymore. I wasn't strong enough.

I hugged everyone as I headed out and back down to the lobby. Although there were lots of people present, I felt as if I were all alone. I somberly greeted those that came to see Caleb for the last time. Loma Linda had brought food for us, so it allowed us to focus solely on one another. Everyone was engaged through talking, crying or simply hugging one another. I think we were all in disbelief that Caleb was actually gone. Nikki approached me and smiled. I thanked her for going up with me and conveyed that God couldn't have chosen a better person for me to share that moment with. John came over and asked if I was ok and I replied that I was the best I could be at that moment. I in return asked him if I could tell him something he said sure. I said, "You'll NEVER be able to hurt me or Caleb ever again!" He stated that he was sorry for all the ways he'd hurt us and that hopefully someday I'd find it in my heart to forgive him. With that he hugged me and slowly walked away.

The hour was late, and I knew that we had to go. I just

couldn't fathom having to depart from the hospital for the final time without my baby. There was no sense in prolonging the matter, so I simply arose and waved goodbye. In order to avoid having to face everyone, we decided not to go home but instead to return to the room that Camille had booked for us. Ryan however, heard the news and met us at the hotel room. I asked him if he would preach at Caleb's service and he agreed without hesitation.

He said, "Remember when we talked about Caleb preaching his biggest message to all of us without even saying a word? Well that's what I'm going to preach at his service." After Ryan left we struggled with the reality that Caleb was actually gone. The girls were laying on my bed at the hotel trying to hold it together. We reminisced on all the great times we had with him and reflected on how blessed we were to have been chosen to receive such a special gift. My phone was ringing off the hook with everyone checking on us. Social media pages were flooded with shock and disbelief that Caleb had lost his battle. He had always came back in the past, but this time he wouldn't. God called my precious baby home. Happy Re-birthday son!

11

REBIRTH

I couldn't sleep I was on Facebook seeing all the outpour of love it was so amazing. So many praying and sending their love, it was so great to see. I couldn't believe that Caleb had touched so many the way he did. He inspired so many to keep going even when times are tough. Caleb was a true hero to so many especially me. And the reality that our hero was gone was very difficult to comprehend. I was having a very hard time wrapping my head around all the things that had gone on and the fact that my baby was gone. I knew he was in Heaven and whole but still I am his mama. I loved him with every part of my being. Everything I did was Caleb Anthony. Now what was my life going to be without him? What was I going to do now that half my heart just died? Not that I wanted him back here definitely not in that body just the fact my heart was shattered into a thousand pieces. My baby was gone, and he was never coming back. I could never hold him again. That for anyone is a very heavy weight to bare!

I didn't get much rest. We all got up and started packing getting ready for our drive home. My heart was very heavy. I was longing for and missing my baby boy! How was I going to walk in that house and face the world now? I felt so empty and lost. I asked Ashley to post on Facebook that is was ok for anybody that wanted to stop by. I knew we needed to be surrounded by all the love and support. We drove up to the house and as crazy as it may sound I couldn't wait to get inside I wanted to feel close to Caleb and what better place than his Heart Home. As we drove up there was a picture on the window of an Olaf with wings that read Heaven's Angel we love and miss you Caleb. There were lit candles under the picture. There a was plant from the fire department on the door step.

I opened the door and walked in. There was a very weird silence. I was glad to be home. We unloaded the car and settled in. My friend Olivia and her daughter were the first to come by. We had only met Olivia a short time before that. She had lost her sweet baby girl a few months prior. I couldn't even imagine what she was going through she was living my worst nightmare. When we met, I didn't know her, but I saw she had lost Lauren and got a hold of some of her family members. I asked if it would be ok if I bring some things by. Oliva said it would be ok, so Caleb and I went to the store and then headed to their home. Caleb and I went in their home and of course Caleb turned on his charm. He had everyone smiling and laughing. We all sat at the table and ate some of the goodies we had brought. After that Caleb and Tommy went outside and hit balls for hours while Olivia sat inside and talked. I kept checking on Caleb and Tommy said that it was ok it was actually helping him because that is what Lauren and he would do all the time. I was glad that Caleb could bring some happiness in such a difficult time of their life. We all just enjoyed one another's company that day! Now they were here doing the same for me! It was so nice to see them. They brought goodies as well. We embraced so hard and now I knew exactly what she was feeling. Man, who would have known just a few months later I would know this? I was thankful to have them here.

Not many people came by that day. I think it was probably hard for them as well because what do you say to someone who just lost their young child? The girls were there, and we just hung out and loved on each other. I was trying to make arrangements to get Caleb out of the morgue at Loma Linda. I hated the idea that he was there but found out that he would have to stay there till Monday. I hated that idea. I didn't want him in there. But there was nothing I could do till Monday. It was hard to believe I was planning my son's Celebration of Life. I wanted it to be magical. I wanted it to be a great celebration. Caleb lived life with such a contagious smile and a crazy zeal and I wanted his last Celebration to be the greatest not for him but for all who attended. We started putting ideas together on how we could do that. I called Robin and she got right on it. She put it out on Facebook that we all would be meeting at Denny's to get the plans together. She was such a life saver especially because I didn't know exactly what to do with myself. I knew the girls and others were watching me. I didn't want to fall apart. I knew God's grace is sufficient to get you through this and if

Caleb could be brave with all he went through then so could I. That night I got a knock on my door it was my neighbor Sherry. She asked me to come outside that her and her family had put together a little tribute for Caleb. It was an angel, it said we love you Caleb. It was lit up with lights! It was amazing! We all hugged and cried. I kept thanking her over and over for doing such a special thing for Caleb. What a very nice way to end a very difficult day.

People were starting to come by more. Lisa, Johanna, Sherry, Melissa, Robin, Julie our Mayor, Barbara, and many others. John and his brother stopped by, so we could get the times and dates for Caleb's celebration. Everyone was there for us in support. John and I talked we discussed a few dates but decided that March 30 would be best to give people ample time to make arrangements and attend. As John and I were talking I saw two girls walking up. It was time for school to be out, so I thought it was just parents walking by. As they approached the door it finally registered in my mind that it was my cousins from Arizona, Heather and Noel. I was so shocked I hadn't seen them in years. We all were so happy to see one another. We hugged and cried. My cousin Melissa and her daughter Scarlett were here. It was like a little family reunion. Sad it was under this circumstance, but we were all very happy to see one another. John was still here, and we had a few things to go over. We agreed on everything and he went home.

My family and friends all sat around and just tried to comfort each other. There was still a very big piece missing and that was Caleb. Even though it was great seeing everyone all I could think about was Caleb in that cold dark morgue. I just wanted to get him out of there. I felt helpless and the reality was he was there. I tried to go to sleep but was having a hard time. I knew the next day I would be heading to the mortuary to sign papers to finalize everything. I was glad Hannah and Ashley stayed with me though. It was so nice to have them there.

I got up early and got ready to go to the mortuary. There was some confusion about where we would meet. We ended up having to go to San Bernardino, CA instead of Victorville, CA. It didn't matter to me as long as we could get Caleb out of that morgue and to the funeral home it was ok with me. I talked with John on the phone and of course we started arguing. I didn't want to deal with that on top of everything else, so I decided to not to talk to him until things were all taken care of. We headed to San Bernardino, CA to take care of things. We got to the funeral home which ironically was right down the street from Loma Linda hospital where Caleb was. I was glad because that meant once we got everything signed they could go right away and get him. We sat down and talked about Caleb and showed the funeral director pictures and videos, so she could know what Caleb was like when he was still alive. They all were very happy to see him and of course fell in love. We talked and got everything finalized. I signed everything.

I asked the director if she could separate Caleb in half so that John and I could have half each. He was our son and that only seemed right. I told them that Caleb had a pacemaker. The funeral director told me they would remove it before he would be cremated. While I was there John kept calling and calling because of the conversation earlier I choose not to answer but I knew him. I knew once I talked with him he was going to be very angry. In the past I would get so nervous but now it wasn't about us it was about Caleb.

We were done, and it was time to head back. We stopped in Victorville, CA I wanted to go by" Things Remembered" so I could find something to keep Caleb's ashes in. We looked around and I found the perfect thing it was a heart shaped music box. It was the perfect choice since my half a heart baby's ashes to be in. When we filled out the paperwork the clerk's face was a little puzzled. I asked what was wrong she said I think his dad was just in here. He just picked out the piece he was going to put his son in and the name is the same. I got a little nervous and wanted to leave because I still hadn't talked with him and I knew if we ran into one another it wasn't going to be a pleasant conversation. While we were still in the store we found this angel piece that was beautiful Ashley loved it to, so we purchased that as well.

On the way home, I decided to call John and of course he was very upset. He was yelling at me as I explained to him that I had taken care of everything all he had to do was go sign his part of the paperwork so that when Caleb's ashes were ready he could go pick them up. He asked about the death certificate I said I already took care of everything. He was so upset and yelling he said my signature needs to be on there. I explained that they only needed one and it was taken care of. He wanted to know where Caleb was I told him they were getting things together and that as soon as he was at the home they would call me and let me know. He was so angry. I told him earlier where and what time I was going he didn't say anything. I told John I just wanted Caleb out of the morgue and now they were on their way to get him. I told John this isn't the time for this I'm sorry you feel the way you do but it's done now. I told him I would let him know when Caleb was at the home. I couldn't handle him yelling at me, so I hung up. John and I had problems like this in the past but for him to act like this now made no sense to me.

We finally got home and got the call Caleb was at the home. The funeral director said he had his very own little spot and was ok. I was so relieved. She also mentioned how adorable he was! That made my heart happy. I texted John and told him Caleb was there. He said he knew he had already contacted the home himself. Guess he needed to check to see if I was telling the truth. However, it was taken care of and Caleb was out of the morgue and resting in the funeral home.

The next few days were very difficult planning and just trying to wrap our heads around the fact Caleb was gone. Family and friends stopped by and brought food. They all made sure we were doing well. We were trying to get everything together so that Caleb's Celebration of Life would be perfect. We were thinking should we let go of birds, but then it hit me what about butterflies that would be so amazing. We got on the internet and looked around. We found this company not too far away. I ordered them so that they would be here the day of the service. Robin was amazing, she got everything and everyone together for the meeting.

We all meet at Denny's. My friends and family and John's friends and family came together. We all threw together ideas of what we thought would be best. I knew it was going to be Frozen themed and Frozen colors. I knew Caleb would love that. Everyone was so supportive. I had been looking on

Pinterest for ideas of what I thought Caleb would love. We all got our thoughts and ideas together and now to make it happen. I love all my friends and family #teamcaleb came together to make my baby's last Celebration amazing!

After we were all done we went back to my house. Melissa Gabe's mom came up and told me about what Gabe had told her. Gabe told her to tell me that Caleb told him to tell me not to cry and that when I'm sleeping Caleb rubs my head with his wings. Gabe mind you is five. He also told Melissa tell her that his wings don't have blood in them anymore that they are pure white because he is now whole now. Man, I was so overwhelmed with that. How precious was that to think my baby boy rubbing my head while I sleep with his wings and that they were pure white and whole. That was the most special thing ever.

Samantha my niece went on to say that when it had gotten dark she went to go get Nathan her son because it was getting dark. Nathan didn't like the dark. Sam told Nathan don't you want to come in now it's dark aren't you scared? Mind you he's three. He said no mom Caleb's playing with me! Sam said oh he is with a little shock? She asked him what's he saying? Nathan replied he's not talking he's just smiling at me! I was so amazed that these two little boys would say something like that. It made my heart full of joy to know that Caleb was still very much around.

I called the funeral home because I was curious about when Caleb would be ready for his service. I really wanted him to be there. The director said there were several clients that had to go before him but assured me that Caleb would be at his service. I was relieved to hear that. John wanted to be in charge of the handouts so Ashley, Marianne, Nathan, and I met him at the printing place that was preparing them. John wanted my approval as well. I went in to look at them. There was a big version and a smaller version. I really like the smaller version and so did John, so we decided on that. Nathan was there and in

Caleb's car seat. Ashley had rolled down the window so that he could look outside. As we were coming out John noticed, and his face looked as if he had seen a ghost. He looked at me and said please have them roll up the window I can't handle that right now! It dawned on me that Nathan was sitting where Caleb had sat. And they were about the same size. I apologized not thinking about that and had them roll up the window.

We got in the car and headed back to Barstow. Hill Billy called and told me that he and the Ranch Riders had been talking. They wanted to do a last ride for Caleb from the Ranch into his Celebration of Life. Hilly Billy asked if that would be ok? We both started to cry and of course I said yes, I would be honored. It was perfect because we all knew Caleb loved motorcycles. Hill Billy was the one who gave him his first ride, so it would be perfect if he also gave him his last ride. I thanked him for all that he had done for Caleb while he was here and now I was thanking him for the wonderful thing he was going to do for him now that he was gone. Hill Billy said it is a privilege and honor. I asked him if he would speak at his service once he got Caleb there. He said of course I will. He was crying and said that is the greatest honor ever. I told him how much I loved him and how thankful I was for him and the whole entire Ranch family!

As soon as I hung up the phone with him I called Allison (who is the owner of the Ranch) and I asked her if she would say something at Caleb's service as well. She said Oh Cathyleen I would love to! We both cried because we loved that little boy so much! I thanked her and told her how much I loved her. I explained that I could never repay her for all she had done for us, but I was so thankful that we had met her. I knew Caleb's service was going to be perfect.

I got the call from the funeral home that Caleb was ready for pickup. I know it sounds crazy, but I was very excited that I would be able to bring Caleb home. I called John and told him that Caleb was ready. John said that he didn't think he could go there. I told him that I would go and that we could meet up somewhere in Victorville. John agreed to that. Marianne and I went down there to pick him up. When we got there, we were talking to the director. She told me about the removal of Caleb's pacemaker. She told me that right before they were going to take him into the crematorium they all stood around Caleb. Held his hand and said a prayer before the removal. As they removed it they sang a song. I started to cry how special was that. I couldn't be there, so they made sure my baby boy was surrounded by love and prayers. That was so amazing.

I asked the director if she was the one who did the cremation? She said that she got too involved and couldn't do it. She told me I fell in love with your special little boy. She went on to tell me even the owner had a difficult time because Caleb was so adorable.

She brought out Caleb's ashes. To my surprise Caleb's ashes were pure white and looked like beach sand. It was crazy I thought about what Gabe had said about Caleb's wings and how they were pure white. Also, at our first appointment I told the director about Caleb. I told her his height and weight she said Caleb was probably going to be about 3 maybe 4 ounces. Well to all our surprise Caleb was much more. The director said remember I said it would depend on Caleb's bone density? She said Caleb's bones were very good. I had a very proud mom moment. Because Caleb was very thin the doctors always said that I needed to work on getting weight on him. Lord knows I tried. Caleb's bones said just that.

I called John and we picked the spot where we would have met. John and big John met us at the place. John looked very stressed out and emotionally drained. He got out of the car and gave me a big hug. He asked me how I was doing? I said I'm ok just working on making Caleb's day amazing. I asked how he was doing and that's when he told me that he was struggling. He said he was having anxiety attacks and having a hard time sleeping. He told me I can't even go home Cathy I've been staying at my Aunt Erica's house. I told him how sorry I was and that I had been praying for him. John said thank you. I asked if he was ready to see Caleb's ashes he replied not really but let's do this. I got Caleb out and showed him both portions. John was tripping out about the fact that they were pure white and looked like beach sand. That's when I proceeded to tell him what Gabe had told Melissa to tell me. John asked how old Gabe was and I told him five. He said that's a trip. Then I told him what Nathan had said. John said that's crazy. I told him it just feels good to know Caleb is still around. As we were leaving John asked me again if I was ok. I told him that I was doing ok in spite of all that is going on. I know where Caleb is and I'm just glad I was able to be his mother. We hugged.

We headed back to Barstow. On the way home Marianne and I talked. I asked her what do you think about putting Caleb in the Olaf? Marianne immediately said I think that would be so cool. As soon as we got home that's exactly what we did. Marianne cut a hole and that's where we put his ashes. It was perfect. I called Hill Billy and asked if it would be ok if I brought Caleb over, so he would be with him and ready for his last ride? He said sure come on over, Marianne and I headed back to Victorville to drop Caleb off. Once we were there Hill Billy hugged me so tight. As we talked we all were very tearful, but they were thanking me for sharing such an extraordinary little boy with them. They also thanked me for the privilege of allowing them to do the last ride for Caleb. We all hugged very tightly, and Marianne and I had to get back, so we could go to the florist and make the final arrangements.

When we got back we headed to the florist and Theresa the owner was telling me her plans for the arrangement. She showed me the colors of the flowers she had ordered. Marianne and I had already been to Walmart to pick up the picture that we wanted in the middle of the arrangement. We picked the picture of Caleb in his Olaf costume at his last birthday. It was going to be so beautiful. I also brought the heart and the angel that we had purchased earlier. Everything was coming together. Caleb's Celebration of Life was going to be perfect. One last thing was balloons. Caleb loved balloons, so I called John and asked his thoughts. He said perfect Cathy, Caleb would love that. I called and ordered them. I started to weep Caleb's service and repass was going to be so perfect.

I received a call from Ashley telling me that I needed to get home. Marianne and I rushed home when I walked in the door my very close childhood friend and Caleb's Godmother was sitting in my living room. Oh, how happy was I to see Kym. Even though she lived on the other side of the United States she has always been my rock through all of this. We didn't make eye contact because we knew if we did we would break down and start crying. We just made small talk and got ready for dinner everyone was coming over. So many family and friends came over and we ate and laughed just reminiscing about life and of course Caleb.

The day before the Celebration we had so much to get done. Everything was coming together. Before we went up to the community center Kym and I stopped by Print & Play they made t-shirts that had Caleb's picture of him in his Olaf costume. They said Team Caleb and had the #3. They were perfect. Chris was so amazing all I could do was cry and thank him. It was time to meet at the community center. We all got there and to our surprise all the tables were set up. They even hung the lights from the ceiling for Caleb. It was going to be so magical. We all started setting up what we had but John had put her in charge of the tables and the centerpieces. She was running very late. We tried to make the best of it. She finally arrived and we all started getting things decorated.

Kym and I had to go to the Barstow Church of God in Christ

to talk about the service and how we would run it. We were talking and getting all the details together. It was going to be perfect. Kisha was there I asked her if she would sing Take Me to The King? She said of course I will Cathyleen, I loved your sweet little boy. It was going to be an amazing Celebration. During the meeting I received a call from Erica telling me that I needed to get back to the community center that she was making decisions and trying to cut out things everyone else knew John and I wanted. I told her we were finishing up and I would be there shortly. I thanked Pastor Norman and everyone else for all their love and support during this difficult time. Pastor Norman said a prayer and Kym and I headed to the community center.

Once I got there, there was a lot of tension in the air. I walked in and said I don't know what's going on but there would absolutely be balloons. John and I already decided that, and they are ordered. They will be here tomorrow. I headed to the kitchen and was talking with my friends. Robin was very upset and was explaining to me what was happening. I couldn't believe my ears all my friends and family had volunteered their time and money and for her to be so rude and disrespectful was very uncalled for especially the day before my son's funeral. Needless to say, I was very upset. I headed out and into her direction. Ashley saw me and said mom you should just go home we can handle the rest. I didn't want to leave because I was very upset. I was going to talk to her but that's when Kym came up and said let's go. I calmed myself down and left with Kym but all the while I couldn't believe she would act like that in a time like this. I got on the phone and talked to John. I told him that he needed to take care of that. I told him what had happened and that she made Robin cry because of her actions. I told him that if she was going to act like that she would not be allowed at the service tomorrow! John took care of it. She called and apologized to Robin. I apologized to Robin as well. But we just moved past that and focused on making sure Caleb's Celebration would be perfect.

Today was the day we all were getting ready to Celebrate the life of our precious Caleb. It was definitely going to be a very emotional day. As I was getting ready I was praying for God's grace to surround me and to flow through me. We got ready and headed to the church. The Church was filling up very quickly. I couldn't believe how many people were there already. Ryan took John and I in the back to talk and pray with us before the service started. John hugged me and said I looked beautiful. I asked how he was doing? He said before I got there, I wasn't sure if I was going to be able to do this but then it hit me how proud I was of my son. Not that I wasn't always proud of him, but it hit me I was so proud of him for all the things he endured that if he could do that then I could do this. That was a great way to look at it I told him.

Ryan came in and had a talk with us. He said let's be nice and make sure no one is mean and disrespectful to anyone because I know the tension between both sides. This is about Caleb and if anyone on either side acts up they will have to leave. We both agreed and then Ryan said you know I love you guys and must look out for you guys right now. It's not about anyone else than you and John and of course the celebration of Caleb's life. We prayed and headed back out the sanctuary. John and I were so surprised the church was full and there were still people lined up to get in. John and I went to the front of the church. We were waiting for Caleb to get there. We were greeting all those that were coming in. Then I heard it! The rumble of the Harley's coming up to the church. I got so excited Caleb's here.

As they pulled up the roar of the engines made the whole church rattle. John and I rushed outside to watch then drive up. The energy was so high as they all parked their bikes. I hugged

Russell he was the president of
the Ranch riders.

I noticed Bridget snapping
pictures she had volunteered to
follow the riders and capture the
moments till they got to the
church. I hugged her so tight
and thanked her. Then Hill Billy
and I locked eyes. He had my precious little boy in his hands.
We embraced like no other hug I had ever had before. It was
happening the reality was that we were all there to say our final
goodbye to Caleb. I held Caleb so tight and John held on to me.
We headed in the church and we carried Caleb up to the front.
It wasn't supposed to happen like that Allison and Hill Billy were
supposed to carry him up there and then do their speeches. But
God had a different plan. I placed Caleb on the table with all the
flowers and other things we had sat on the table. John hugged
me so tight and we cried. Then we sat down.

Latron started to sing. Jesus love the little children. He put a
little twist on it. It was perfect. After he was done Malcolm
started the service. He prayed and then invited Allison and Hill
Billy up to the podium. They both had such nice things to say
about Caleb. Hill Billy talked about the first time he met him
and how much it meant to him to give him his first ride and how
honored he was to give him his last. Allison talked about the first
time she got to meet him and how he stole her heart at the first
sight. They both spoke and were having a very difficult time
holding back their tears, but they got through it. As they went
back to their seats they stopped and hugged me and told me how
much they loved me. They thanked me again for sharing such a
special light with them. Malcolm said some more words and
then it was time for Ms. Muir, Caleb's teacher to come. She
immediately said I don't know if I can do this! I love that little
boy so much. She looked up and said this is for you Caleb. Ms.

Muir told a story about how Caleb was being very stubborn one day and she was trying to get him to write something on the paper. Caleb took the paper, put it in his mouth and started eating it. She said I wasn't sure what to do at that moment, so she picked up another piece of paper and put it her mouth. Ms. Muir said that she and Caleb laughed so hard. She ended her speech with "I love you Caleb and I'm so glad I got to be your teacher".

Next was the PowerPoint Ashley made. She picked the songs best day ever by Sponge Bob and then she picked I lived by One Republic. As the songs played and all the different moments went by. All I could think is how Caleb had a great life and how he did live. Even though it was only 9 1/2 years he did more than most do in a lifetime. Caleb lived with a smile and with so much joy. His smile lit up a room and if you had the privilege of being in his presence you definitely didn't walk away the same. He always had a smile even in the worst of times. That's what Caleb taught me smile through it all! When it's good smile, and when it's bad smile! How blessed I was to have such a brave courageous boy with half a heart. He made everyone's heart he met whole and gave them strength to face another day.

Next was Big John. He said I'm not sure how to follow that. He said that the video touched him. Big John said I wished that I could have seen Caleb like that living life. He went on to explain that he really only saw him when he was in the hospital because they lived so close to Stanford. He said but that is something I will always have to live with. He said life is so precious take advantage of the moment because it can be over, and you never get that time back. Big John went on to read his obituary.

Next was Kisha to sing Take Me to The King. She was choked up at first then the Holy Spirit filled her up. I have never heard her sing like that before. I stood up praising and thanking the Lord for Caleb. The Holy Ghost was moving and lifted me up. He gently laid me on the floor. As I was on the floor I was just crying out to the Lord. I was thanking Him for allowing me to be Caleb's mother. I regrouped myself and sat back down.

Malcolm invited anyone to say a few words. Sharonda came and spoke about the last time she had saw Caleb and how happy he was. Mrs. Beal talked about how every time she saw Caleb he was always happy and enjoyed her cooking, and Juan he said how much he loved Caleb. It was time for Ryan to speak. He preached his little heart out. Ryan told a little background about how he met John and me. He said it was because of him and his sister Sharonda that we met. Then he went into the sermon about Caleb and his life. He preached about how Caleb had little words but spoke very loudly. He had everyone look around the room and notice all the different people. There were bikers, every race, police officers, firefighters, skinny people, big people, but no matter what you were or looked like Caleb loved you for you. And that's the lesson we should take from Caleb and his life is to love hard and unconditionally. The words Ryan preached pierced everyone's heart and soul. Ryan did such a great job.

Once Ryan was finished my cousin Melissa and I got up we had a very special gift to present to John. My cousin had, in four short days made John a blanket out of Caleb's t-shirt's and his Baseball uniform. John got up and accepted the blanket. Then thanked us and hugged the blanket so tight. The service was over now it was time to go to the community center. I walked in and it was so beautiful! Exactly what I hoped it would be. There were already so many people. I walked around and greeted everyone. Lisa's husband Mike was the announcer. My dear friend Michael was DJ. There was so much food. So many restaurants around Barstow made sure we had everything. Dinapolis, Los Domingo's, David my brother sent food from the Olive Garden, and everyone else cooked their special dish for Caleb. As the people came in the community center was filling up. I was so overwhelmed to see all these people some familiar and some I had never seen before coming to celebrate Caleb's life. It was crazy to me that people kept coming up to me saying you don't know me but... I follow you and Caleb's story. They said it gave them so much hope and inspiration. It kept happening over and over again. I was trying to make sure I didn't forget to thank every single person that was there.

They finally made me sit down and eat I am not kidding I only took about ten minutes and then I was back up greeting people again. John and I got up and thanked everyone for coming and celebrating Caleb's life with us. I had a surprise I asked everyone to meet us outside the back of the community center. Once we were out there I told everyone that I had butterflies and that we were going to let them go for Caleb. Derane said a prayer and then I proceeded to let them go. It was a very chilly day so some of them flew off, but the others were still kind of frozen, so I tried to help them fly but unfortunately, they just fell on the ground. Not what I was hoping for, but the kids got excited and got them. Somehow one of the butterflies got stuck in my hair. It was funny Somebody said that Caleb wasn't quite ready to leave you yet. I smiled because that was a very nice thought especially on a day like that.

I went into the kitchen to thank all my girls in there. Suzy, Raylene, Tracey, Ann Marie, Jenna, Fran, Diane, and Robin. I noticed that on the food David had sent said #Teamcaleb. I hugged all of them and thanked them so much for all they had done. That's when they told me that one of the butterflies ended up in there with them. That was so crazy Caleb flew in there to give them a special thank you.

I went to the table where Camille, Jennifer, and a few other nurses were sitting to thank them for coming. That's when Jennifer gave me a gift. I opened it, it was a giving key. She explained what it was that this company took homeless people and gave them a job to help them got off the streets. They engraved different words on the keys. Mine read courage. Jennifer said I know from here on out you're going to need a lot of courage to rebuild your life after Caleb, so you wear this key. And when you're ready your supposed to pass it on to the next person and tell them your story and why you have decided to give it to them. Then go to the website and write your story. I thanked her, and the tears started flowing that was a special key and how honored I was to receive it.

It was time to clean up now. There was so much food leftover that we told people to take plates home. Even after that so much ended up at my house. We all sat and reflected on the day it was so amazing. It was the perfect way to celebrate such a special little boys life. I was so thankful for all those and all those who couldn't be there who reached out on Facebook. It was so nice to think of how many people Caleb touched and how many loved him. Team Caleb Rocks!

That night after the celebration Ashley told me about the what had happened at the hospital after the nurse called and said we had forgotten Caleb's feet and handprints. She asked if someone could come up there and get it. Ashley said she would go. Not knowing when she got up there that Caleb was still in there. Ashley went on to tell me that when she walked in she was so surprised because Caleb's face was white as a ghost. She started to cry as she was telling me this. I asked her what did you do? She said mom I couldn't just leave him he's my brother, so I went over to the bed and kissed him and told him how much I loved him. I told her that moment was only for you Ashley. Think of all the stuff we have heard from Gabe and Nathan and how Caleb was whole and happy. Now think about Caleb's ashes being pure white. That moment with you and your brother was very special he was showing you that now he was whole and pure. He was an angel now and I think that's what the white represents. Ashley was crying and said that makes sense mom. I could tell she felt better.

I had applied for unemployment and was waiting for the letter for my claim. I had set up accounts on all the different websites to look for jobs. I redid my resume, but it wasn't looking too hot because the only thing I had done for the past ten years was care for Caleb and run a non-profit. I was taught in school you really are only supposed to go back ten years. So, I did the best I could. I finally received the letter from the unemployment office that read I didn't qualify because of some code that stated because I was the parent of the patient I was excluded. I was in shock. I don't qualify because I was his mother? I called the unemployment office immediately. I was on hold for quite some time, but my call was finally connected there was a worker on the end named Tracy. I asked her if I misread the letter? She went on to explain that no in fact that I read it correctly if you're an In Home Supportive Service worker and you take care of your child or spouse you are excluded but all other recipients qualify up to 26 weeks. I started to cry. I told Tracey all that I had been through during Caleb's life and how I was looking for employment, to help me until I could find a job. I didn't have much relative work skills because I cared for Caleb I wasn't getting any feedback except another candidate has been selected. Tracey and I talked for a long time. She told me that she hated this part of her job. To tell someone like me that had just lost their child that there was no money coming was the hardest thing to do. I said how do we change this. Tracey said it's a law, the only way to change it is to change the law. I told her I was going to appeal it because that wasn't fair. She said that was a great idea. But again, it's a law you have to change the law. Ok let's try to change the law and appeal as far as I could go at the same time.

Ok where do I start?

———

To Be Continued....

CONCLUSION

Caleb's story is encompassed with lots of emotions and lessons. During his nine years on this earth Caleb had some very great moments and some very devastating moments. Throughout it all Caleb was a hero. He endured things in his nine years that most won't throughout a whole life time. I could have written the book to teach you what I learned from Caleb's journey, but God revealed to me in my spirit that everyone that reads this book will learn something different. Each one of you will have the pleasure of God tapping into your deepest emotions depending on where you are in your very special walk in this life. Whatever you learn whether it be courage, to believe, forgiveness, strength, longsuffering, patience, endurance, hope, whatever it is I believe once you walk away from Caleb's story you will be forever changed for the good. I believe that Caleb's story will encourage you to look at life differently and to embrace each moment with all your heart and soul. I believe it will teach you to never take one moment for granted and to love the ones God has blessed you with as if this day would be their last.

Caleb taught me to embrace life regardless of what it takes

you through. Caleb was the strongest person I knew. Some people search all their life for a hero to follow or to look up to. I had the honor and privilege of giving birth to mine. Caleb was a quiet hero that overcame so much and in the most painful times found a way to smile through it all. Caleb had a very simple life but every single person he met was impacted somehow.

Despite all the hurts and betrayal, we encountered during this journey, I have somehow became so thankful for it! Without that I would have never tapped into my inner-strengths and been able to accomplish the things I was able to, to ensure Caleb could live his best life while he was here. And still working so hard to make sure that children and adults like him can live their best lives.

Sometimes in life we wonder why? Caleb taught me stop asking why and live! Live, Caleb lived and loved with his whole heart even though he only had half! My little half of a heart baby impacted so many and will continue to! Embrace life with a smile! Give it all you've got and know that no matter what, it will all eventually work out for the good in the end!

PHYSICIAN LIST

1. Dr. A—Pediatric Neurologist
2. Dr. AL—Pediatric Cardiologist
3. Dr. B—Thoracic and Cardiac Surgeon-Pediatric Cardiologist
4. Dr. C—Obstetrics and Gynecology
5. Dr. G—Pediatric Cardiologist
6. Dr. H—Chief Pediatric Cardiac Surgery
7. Dr. KO—Pediatric Pulmonologist
8. Dr. LB—Thoracic and Cardiac Surgeon
9. Dr. M—Chief of Pediatric Cardiology
10. Dr. O—Obstetrics and Gynecology, Chief of Maternal-Fetal Medicine
11. Dr. P—Internist
12. Dr. R—Thoracic and Cardiac Surgeon
13. Dr. RW—Otolaryngology Physician-Ear, Nose, and Throat
14. Dr. S—Pediatric Cardiologist
15. Dr. SP—Pediatric Cardiology Specialist
16. Dr. T—Obstetrics and Gynecology

17. Dr. W—Pediatric Cardiology

ABOUT THE AUTHOR

Cathyleen Williams (Wilson) was born in Barstow California, the younger of two children. After a school career that included some time in private school, she married young and had a daughter named Ashley.

While trying to find herself, Cathyleen went on to wed a few more times eventually settling down with John Lucas who she bore a son with. Her son was born with hypoplastic left heart syndrome or as Cathyleen would say, her son was born with half a heart.

Cathyleen was the full-time care provider for Caleb who, in 2016 earned his wings. As a result, Cathy founded a non-profit organization rightly titled Babies So Special.

When Cathyleen isn't working her full-time job at On the Rise, she is organizing fundraisers for her non-profit. helping the special needs community is her passion. Cathyleen's moto is "Give a voice to the voiceless" which she strives to do every day.

Made in the USA
Middletown, DE
23 March 2019